TRAVERSE THEATRE

presents the world premiere of

SHINING SOULS

By Chris Hannan

Director	Ian Brown
Designer	**Frank Gerssen** *prizewinner 1995 Linbury Prize for Stage Design*
Lighting Designer	Chahine Yavroyan
Composer	John Irvine
Assistant Director	John Tiffany
Movement Director	Caroline Salem
Margaret Mary	Mabel Aitken
Prophet John	Frank Gallagher
Mandy	Molly Innes
Billy 1	Tom McGovern
Charlie	Stuart McQuarrie
Nanette	Anne Myatt
Ann	Alison Peebles
Stuart / Vince	John Ramage
Billy 2	John Stahl
Max	Finlay Welsh

First performed at the Traverse Theatre
Thursday 8 August 1996

Sponsored by
The
Linbury
Trust

TRAVERSE
THEATRE

This production is sponsored by the Linbury Trust

TRAVERSE THEATRE

Over the last three decades Edinburgh's Traverse Theatre has had a seminal influence on British and international theatre. With quality, award-winning productions and programming, the Traverse receives accolades at home and abroad from audiences and critics alike.

Traverse productions have been seen world-wide. After sell-out Edinburgh runs MOSCOW STATIONS transferred to both the West End and to New York, Off Broadway. UNIDENTIFIED HUMAN REMAINS AND THE TRUE NATURE OF LOVE and POOR SUPER MAN transferred to Hampstead Theatre, and after touring the Highlands and Islands of Scotland, KNIVES IN HENS transferred to a sell-out season at the Bush Theatre in London. This year Sue Glover's BONDAGERS toured the world, delighting audiences in Edinburgh, London, Toronto and Budapest.

The Traverse is a power-house of quality experimentation, artistic diversity and the place to see some of the most important contemporary theatre work around. The Theatre commissions the best new writers from Scotland and around the world; facilitates numerous script development workshops, rehearsed readings and public writing workshops; and produces six major new theatre productions plus a Scottish touring production each year. An essential element of the Company's activities takes place within the educational sector, concentrating on the process of new writing in schools. The Traverse is unique in its exclusive dedication to new writing – providing the infrastructure, professional support and expertise to ensure the development of a sustainable and relevant theatre culture for Scotland.

For the 1996 Festival the Traverse presents both the world premiere of Chris Hannan's SHINING SOULS and David Greig's THE ARCHITECT, which returns to the Traverse stage following its tremendous success in the Spring.

TRAVERSE THEATRE

CHRIS HANNAN: His plays include KLIMKOV (Traverse 1984), ELIZABETH GORDON QUINN (Traverse 1985), THE ORPHAN'S COMEDY (Traverse 1986), THE BABY (Tron 1990), THE EVIL DOERS (Bush 1990). Chris's awards include a Time Out Award, Plays and Players critics Award and Charrington London Fringe Award for Best Play. Current projects include a mountain rescue series for BBC and a novel called THE BIG BORRASCA, set in the American West.

FRAGILE, BROKEN AND DESPERATE

Playwright and actor Simon Donald interviews
CHRIS HANNAN

At the Traverse in 1984 Peter Lichtenfels (then Artistic Director) commissioned three one-act plays. Chris Hannan wrote PURITY – a compact jewel of a piece, allusive, poetic, gnomic – about the precocious young Beethoven. Or it seemed like it might be about the precocious young Beethoven.

The actors were pestering the writers afterwards and I remember Simon Russell Beale cross-examining Chris who I'd only just met and I was eavesdropping and sizing him up, 'cause you know – was this going to be the beginning of a lifelong, venomous rivalry – and Russell Beale was being exquisitely articulate and inciteful and Chris Hannan was going '...eh...uhuh. I mean, ye know, I don't mean ...eh...you know, I mean...' And I thought – no way he wrote that play. His *dad* maybe wrote that play but no way the boy Hannan had a hand in it.

The actors decided the play had come from some hideously deformed genius who couldn't show his real face and consequently had to sub-contract all his public appearances to the youth in ill-fitting jumpers.

And oddly enough that's sort of how it is. I mean there's this Celtic supporter who drinks large vodka and Irn Brus then there's this frightening intellectual who got an Oxford first and was the Machiavellian mastermind behind the only successful playwrights' strike in the history of the British Isles and together they write great plays.

I think his plays to date oscillate around two poles – the populist and the intellectual, and as you look through them in order you can see how he swings one way then back in the other direction with the next – occasionally – as with ELIZABETH GORDON QUINN striking a perfect balance and only once, with THE ORPHAN'S COMEDY getting the mix a bit weird.

THE ORPHAN'S COMEDY was a fiercely complicated and funny play about futures speculating shenanigans in a fertility clinic. It had a plot that was wound as tight as WHAT THE BUTLER SAW and contained some monstrously funny characters and moments and it didn't quite work.

When we talk about it he says that he now doesn't like the things that people liked about it. A bit show-offy.

Maybe it's that THE ORPHAN'S COMEDY doesn't have as much soul as he puts in his best stuff. Like his precocious starting piece PURITY it's too opaque and overwrought.

ELIZABETH GORDON QUINN, THE BABY and THE EVIL DOERS all have in their hearts an emotional incendiary device that sizzles through the play and then catches light. In EGQ it's to do with your parents – in THE BABY it's about a doomed attempt to love and be loved by someone who's filled with rage, and in THE EVIL DOERS it's the carnage and damage that strews around an alcoholic. I'm absolutely not saying they're issue plays and those are the issues because his stuff is far beyond that kind of glib reductionism – just that amongst all the other things that are going on in them, there is a central pulse that's a bit bigger and more devastating and I think it's to do with love. Not Art.

I say that because Chris's plays have a history of dodgy programme notes that tell you the play you're about to see is about something it isn't.

When ELIZABETH GORDON QUINN came out the programme said this play about a woman and her piano was a metaphor for 'Art'. It didn't help that the set and design were alienatingly Brechtian (I know that's the point but it still didn't help). Consequently, the first time round, some people sat there thinking I can see this woman and her family and her piano and I can hear what they're saying but what is it telling me about 'Art'? He says people who knew where it came from weren't seeing metaphors but I was in it and I'd read the programme notes and I found myself asking Bernard Doherty – what does this piano we're humphing across the stage represent again?

Fortunately EGQ has since entered the repertoire and played in theatres like Dundee Rep. and Perth where audiences were able to get into it without any Art in the way.

EVIL DOERS obviously had much better programme notes because it won loads of prizes and went down a storm and it contained a whole host of those moments when an audience goes quiet because they've now got to know a character well enough to sense they're about to see something of their soul.

We talk about audiences a bit. There's this basic question about what you're attempting to do to an audience. He goes 'Um and eh..I mean...' for a bit so I ask him what his best thing in the theatre is. What he's seen that's made him go 'Yup. That's what you try to do'. He takes ages to answer me and I'm worrying he's going to come up with one of those things that you're meant to have seen except you decided to stay in and watch some good telly instead and he says THE STEAMIE. Now I hadn't expected him to come up with THE STEAMIE. If you know the play at all – it's Tony Roper and David Andersons' amazingly popular runaway musical hit which in Scotland is seen as a dead-cert whenever a company needs a money maker. And it's the kind of thing we're all supposed to be snooty about. But he's right.

'THE STEAMIE is a beautiful play. It makes me cry and it's an incredible laugh and there's a tremendous amount of love and loss in it and it's ostensibly nostalgic but it's not really and when you're in the audience it's full of folk who've seen it before but they've brought their pals and they're all completely on for the night and it's set on Hogmanay which is incredibly ritualistic when everybody thinks about their dead and old Mrs Culfeathers says something dead simple about being finished and it's completely heartbreaking and everybody cries...you know what I mean?'

He worries about this a lot – people knowing what he means – his conversations are self-devastated by his own hesitations and interruptions and qualifications. You embark on a dialogue and end up refereeing a kamikaze monologue that gradually spirals down into monosyllables and befuddled facial expressions.

I ask him what SHINING SOULS is. He says it's a Romance.

I ask him what's changed – since SCREW THE BOBBIN his first play, an agit-prop piece for 7:84. Has he grown up, matured, slowed down? What's different?

He says he feels a bit like Charlie, the mess in the middle of SHINING SOULS. I ask him how Charlie feels and he says Charlie is fragile, broken ,and desperate. But quite handsome.

I also ask about the language. Chris was brought up Catholic and his family are all Catholic and the play has passages of intense religious poetry. He says that his characters are desperately testing themselves to find out who they are – if they deserve to have love – if they're allowed to feel love for somebody else. In a way this is religious activity and the poetry he wields in the play is instrumental in trying these fundamental longings. It's how you look into your heart. You could use another language like the language of psychoanalysis but that's not a language he's so fluent in.

SHINING SOULS is one of those few plays that I've read and gone 'Yup. That's what you try to do.'

The closest relative for me is Sam Shepherd. Those two Shepherd plays BURIED CHILD and LIE OF THE MIND – Romances, Emotional Thrillers about Love and Loss. And what they do is make audiences join together and hold their breath and wait for the moment where your throat clenches and the person on stage opens and you see inside.

It's just such a shame though that SHINING SOULS is about Art.

SIMON DONALD

Simon Donald is a prolific actor, playwright, long-term friend and venomous rival of Chris Hannan. Over the last ten years Simon has worked extensively in many theatres, including the Traverse, as an actor and writer. His award-winning play THE LIFE OF STUFF was part of the opening season when the Traverse moved to Cambridge Street; it had a subsequent production at the Donmar Warehouse in London and is being made as a film. Chris Hannan wrote the programme notes.

Simon's recent television work includes Denis Potter's KARAOKE and BAD BOYS for BBC Scotland.

SHINING SOULS was *originally developed for the National Theatre Studio and the Royal Court Theatre. The writer's agent is Alan Brodie c/o Alan Brodie Representation, 21 Piccadilly, London W1V 9LD.*

SHINING SOULS

Margaret Mary	**Mabel Aitken**
Prophet John	**Frank Gallagher**
Mandy	**Molly Innes**
Billy 1	**Tom McGovern**
Charlie	**Stuart McQuarrie**
Nanette	**Anne Myatt**
Ann	**Alison Peebles**
Stuart / Vince	**John Ramage**
Billy 2	**John Stahl**
Max	**Finlay Welsh**

Stage Manager	**Gavin Johnston**
Deputy Stage Manager	**Kay Courteney-Chrystal**
Assistant Stage Manager	**Victoria Paulo**
Wardrobe Supervisor	**Lynn Ferguson**
Wardrobe Assistant	**Alice Taylor**

MABEL AITKEN *(Margaret Mary)*: Trained RSAMD. Theatre work includes: GODODDIN (Test Department); THE CRUCIBLE, UNCLE VANYA, MIRANDOLINA (Royal Lyceum); THE EVIL DOERS (Winged Horse); THE LIFE OF STUFF (Traverse *and* Donmar Warehouse); HUGHIE ON THE WIRES (Calypso); CUTTIN' A RUG (Young Vic); TWO SEVENS CLASH (Damage); ALL IN THE TIMING (Nottingham Playhouse). For radio: THE CONFIDENCE (BBC Scotland); THE BELL IN THE TREE (Radio Clyde). Television work includes: RAB C. NESBITT, NERVOUS ENERGY, BETWEEN THE LINES (BBC); SEARCHING. Film work includes: FEVER PITCH and WANTING AND GETTING.

IAN BROWN *(Director)*: Artistic Director of the Traverse Theatre since 1988. Productions for the Traverse include: STONES AND ASHES *by Daniel Danis*, READER *by Ariel Dorfman*, THE COLLECTION *by Mike Cullen*, AWAY *by Michael Gow*, UNIDENTIFIED HUMAN REMAINS AND THE TRUE NATURE OF LOVE, POOR SUPER MAN *by Brad Fraser* (Traverse / Hampstead), TRAINSPOTTING *adapted by Harry Gibson* (Citizens Theatre), TALLY'S BLOOD *by Ann-Marie di Mambro*, THE HOPE SLIDE *by Joan McLeod*, INES DE CASTRO, A LIGHT IN THE VILLAGE *by John Clifford* (Traverse and BBC TV), MOSCOW STATIONS *adapted by Stephen Mulrine* (Traverse/Garrick), ANNA – AN OPERA *by John Clifford and Craig Armstrong*, BUCHANAN *by Tom McGrath*, LOOSE ENDS *by Stuart Hepburn*, THE HOUSE AMONG THE STARS *by Michel Tremblay*, COLUMBUS *by Michele Celeste*, PIGPLAY *by Raymond Cousse*, THE BENCH *by Alexander Gelman*, THE COW JUMPED OVER THE MOON *by Donna Franceschild* and HARDIE AND BAIRD *by James Kelman*. Ian was formerly Artistic Director of TAG Theatre Company and before that Associate Director of the Theatre Royal Stratford East. In September 1996 he leaves the Traverse to pursue a freelance career.

FRANK GALLAGHER *(Prophet John)*: Trained RSAMD. Theatre work includes: ROAD (7:84); THE APPOINTMENT (Wildcat); THE

SLAB BOYS, LOOT (Lyceum); PLATFORM DOUBLE BILL, POTATO SPIRIT, DEAD PIDGEON BOYS, TARTUFFE (Annexe); WAITING FOR BABY, THE BEAUTIFUL GAME (Gallus); NEW SCOTTISH PLAY READINGS (Tron); JULIUS CAESAR (Opening Acts); HUGHIE ON THE WIRES, THE CUT, BROTHERS OF THE BRUSH (Wiseguise); THE COLLECTION (Traverse); SHADOW OF A GUNMAN, SWING HAMMER SWING (Citizens). Television work includes: DREAM BABY, THE JUSTICE GAME II, JUTE CITY, CITY LIGHTS, RUFFIAN HEARTS (BBC); TAGGART, SUPPERMAN, DR FINLAY. Film work includes: SILENT SCREAM (Silent Scream Ltd); A CHILL (Scottish Film Training Trust); JOYRIDER (BFI); HARD NUT (Prime Cut); INITIATION (Tartan Short). Frank has also worked extensively for BBC Radio Drama and Radio Clyde. Directed THE WISHING TREE (Wiseguise).

FRANK GERSSEN (*Designer*): Born in Holland, trained at The Architectural Association School of Architecture and the Motley Theatre Design Course. In 1995 Frank was a prize winner of the Linbury Prize for Stage Design. Theatre work includes: Assistant designer on: CAPRICIO (Garsington 1994); ARMSTRONG'S LAST GOODNIGHT (Lyceum); THE RAKE'S PROGRESS (Welsh National Opera); LES MISERABLES (Karlstadt, Sweden); Designer BEYOND THERAPY (New End Theatre).

MOLLY INNES (*Mandy*): Theatre work includes: STONES AND ASHES, CROSS DRESSING IN THE DEPRESSION (Traverse); DREAMING IN PUBLIC (Traverse & Byre); DOING BIRD (Cat A Theatre Co.); PLAYBOY OF THE WESTERN WORLD (Communicado); TO KILL A MOCKING BIRD, THE PRIME OF MISS JEAN BRODIE (Lyceum); STINGING SEA (Citizens); TARTUFFE (Dundee Rep); GLORIA GOODHEART AND THE GLITTER GRAB GANG, JOLLY ROBERT AND THE PIRATES FROM SPACE (Theatre Workshop); MURDER AND THE MUSIC HALL (Theatre Public). Television work includes: A MUGS GAME; TAKIN' OVER THE ASYLUM; THE FERGUSON THEORY; STRATHBLAIR; RAB C. NESBITT. Radio work includes: BILL 'N' KOO, SOME OF MY BEST FRIENDS ARE DOLPHINS (BBC Radio Four), THE FOURTH FOREIGNER. Film: STELLA DOES TRICKS.

JOHN IRVINE (*Sound Designer*): Trained RSAMD, University of Edinburgh. Theatre work includes: MOSCOW STATIONS (Traverse, Garrick & Union Square Theatre, New York); POOR SUPERMAN, UNIDENTIFIED HUMAN REMAINS (Traverse & Hampstead), STONES AND ASHES, READER, EUROPE, THE HOPE SLIDE, BROTHERS OF THUNDER, BUCHANAN, THE LIFE OF STUFF, COLUMBUS: BLOODING THE OCEAN, THE STRUGGLE OF THE DOGS AND THE BLACK (Traverse); TRAINSPOTTING (Citizens & Bush Theatre); THE NEW MENOZA (Gate Theatre); RUNNING WITH MY HEAD DOWN (KTC, Tramway); WHITE BIRD PASSES (Dundee Rep); SEVEN-TENTHS (Walk The Plank); WHALE (Cumbernauld); THE BABY (RSAMD) PINNOCHIO (Visible Fictions). Film work includes: DOG DAYS (NFTS).

TOM McGOVERN (*Billy 1*): Trained RSAMD, winner of the *James Bridie Gold Medal*. Theatre work includes: HAMLET, OUR COUNTRY'S GOOD, ARMSTRONG'S LAST GOODNIGHT, OF MICE AND MEN (Lyceum); THE GRAPES OF WRATH, ARTURO UI (7:84); AMERICAN BUFFALO (Dundee Rep); MACBETH, JACK AND THE BEANSTALK (Tron); DR FAUSTUS (Pen Name); THÉRÈSE RAQUIN (Communicado); THE THRIE ESTAITES, THE PASSION (Edinburgh Festival); THE EVIL DOERS (Winged Horse); MAN EQUALS MAN

(Chandler Studio); DON JUAN (Traverse); TWELVE ANGRY MEN (Arches); BENT (Athenaeum); Television work includes: ATHLETICO PARTICK, and PIE IN THE SKY.

STUART McQUARRIE *(Charlie)*: Trained RSAMD. Theatre work includes: CARMEN (Scottish Opera); THE SNOW QUEEN (Dundee Rep); HAYFEVER, THE GLASS MENAGERIE, THE MERCHANT OF VENICE, CHARLIE'S AUNT, DEATH OF A SALESMAN, MOTHER COURAGE, SLAB BOYS, LOOK BACK IN ANGER, THE COUNTRY WIFE, THE COMEDIANS, THE BEVELLERS, ARSENIC AND OLD LACE, GOOD MORNING BILL, LAUREL AND HARDY (Lyceum); A MIDSUMMER NIGHT'S DREAM (TAG); CITY LIGHTS (P.D.B.); LOOSE ENDS, CLOCKED OUT, INES DE CASTRO,(also London) HARDIE AND BAIRD, THE LIFE OF STUFF, THE HOUSE AMONG THE STARS (Traverse); THE THRIE ESTAITES (Edinburgh Festival); MACBETH (Tron and Dundee Rep); THE LIFE OF STUFF (Donmar Warehouse); THE SLAB BOYS TRILOGY (Young Vic); BOYS STUFF (Crucible, Sheffield). Television work includes: THE CONTINENTAL, CHRISTMAS FUN, THE JUSTICE GAME, LOOSE ENDS, INES DE CASTRO, CITY LIGHTS, STRATHBLAIR, SECRETS, HIGH LIFE, HAMISH MACBETH, CASUALTY (BBC); TAGGART, DR FINLAY (STV); THE PETER PRINCIPLE (Hat Trick); LONDON'S BURNING. Film includes: LOVE ME TENDER; TRAINSPOTTING.

ANNE MYATT *(Nanette)*: Theatre work includes: MEN SHOULD WEEP, IN TIME OF STRIFE, THE GORBALS STORY (7:84); ROMEO AND JULIET (TAG); TARTUFFE, MOTHER COURAGE (Lyceum); 'TIS A PITY SHE'S A WHORE, DR ANGELUS, THE ALCHEMIST, THE DOUGLAS, THE CRUCIBLE, THE SORCERER'S APPRENTICE, TALE OF TWO CITIES, GOSPELS, SUMMER LIGHTNING, THE PELICAN, WOMEN BEWARE WOMEN (Citizens); AWAY (Traverse). Among many appearances on Scottish television: HIGH ROAD, TAGGART (STV); CARDIAC ARREST (BBC); CROW ROAD (Union Pictures).

ALISON PEEBLES *(Ann)*: Theatre work includes: INES DE CASTRO; KORA; ORPHAN'S COMEDY (Traverse); MACBETH (Tron). She has also worked extensively throughout the UK with companies including: Royal Exchange, Manchester, Bush, London, Royal National, ATC, Dundee Rep, Royal Lyceum, Citizens, Raindog, Young Vic, Duke's Playhouse, Borderline, Nottingham Playhouse and is an Associate Director with Communicado with whom she has worked on several productions including: CARMEN; MARY QUEEN OF SCOTS GOT HER HEAD CHOPPED OFF; BLOOD WEDDING. Television work includes: THE FINAL CUT; TAGGART; THE ADVOCATES; ALBERT AND THE LION; RAB C NESBITT; CASUALTY; MILES IS BETTER; THE PRIEST AND THE PIRATE; INES DE CASTRO; STRATHBLAIR. Film work includes: BRAVEHEART, MIRROR, MIRROR, THE STAR. Alison has also worked extensively for BBC Radio Drama and Features.

JOHN RAMAGE *(Stuart/Vince)*: Theatre work includes: YOUR TURN TO CLEAN THE STAIRS (Traverse); ELEGIES FOR ANGELS, PUNKS AND RAGING QUEENS (Luckenbooth); THE BOYFRIEND, ROUGH CROSSING, H.M.S. PINAFORE, THE MIKADO (Perth Theatre); NIGHT SKY (Stellar Quines); SALVATION (Tron). John has also been involved in numerous tours as well as fifteen pantomime seasons at King's Theatres (Edinburgh and Glasgow), Sunderland Empire, Tron and the Lyceum. He also directed THE LAST OF THE LAIRDS (Perth Theatre) and is a lecturer in Acting Studies at

Edinburgh's Queen Margaret College where he has directed many productions including SIX DEGREES OF SEPARATION and THE LIFE OF STUFF. Television work includes: THE HIGH LIFE, RAB C. NESBITT. BBC Radio Drama work includes: THE MISANTHROPE, A SONG FOR EUROPE, THE WRONG BOX, BORDER INCIDENT, WHISKEY GALORE.

JOHN STAHL *(Billy 2)*: Trained RSAMD. Theatre work includes: THE BATTLE OF BAREFOOT (Theatre Space); NEXT TIME I'LL SING TO YOU, THE GAME (Edinburgh Festival); ALADDIN, THE CARETAKER, WHAT THE BUTLER SAW, THE GLASS MENAGERIE, ZOO STORY, ENTERTAINING MR SLOANE (Cumbernauld); THE SASH AND THE GAME (Glasgow Pavilion); LENT (Lyric); COMMEDIA (Sheffield Crucible/Lyric/King's, Edinburgh); MACBETH, THE SLEEPING BEAUTY, PADDY'S MARKET, REAL WURLD (Tron); DEATH OF A SALESMAN, THE SNOW QUEEN, THE CRUCIBLE (Lyceum); ALADDIN (Adam Smith); HAMLET, COMEDIANS (Belgrade, Coventry); CINDERELLA (Dundee Rep). Television includes: YOU'RE A GOOD BOY, SON, A SENSE OF FREEDOM, GARNOCK WAY, HIGH ROAD, ALBERT AND THE LION, CRIME STORY, TAGGART (STV); THE McKINNONS, RESORT TO MURDER, PARAHANDY, DR FINLAY (BBC). Film work includes LOCH NESS.

JOHN TIFFANY *(Assistant Director)*: Trained: Glasgow University. Assistant Director at the Traverse since August 1995. He directed SHARP SHORTS, co-directed STONES AND ASHES and was assistant director on THE ARCHITECT for the Traverse. Other work includes: THE SUNSET SHIP (Young Vic); GRIMM TALES (Leicester Haymarket). He set up LOOKOUT, a new writing theatre company, for whom his directing work includes HIDE AND SEEK and BABY, EAT UP which he co-wrote with Vicky Featherstone. He has also worked as a script editor for Ikona Films.

FINLAY WELSH *(Max)*: Theatre includes: THE RAGGED TROUSERED PHILANTHROPISTS, NO MEAN CITY (7:84); PHILADELPHIA HERE I COME, CENTURY'S END, THE WITCHES OF POLLOK (Tron); MONTROSE, THE RIVALS, THE HYPOCHONDRIAK, MOTHER COURAGE, AS YOU LIKE IT, THE BEVELLERS (Lyceum); ONE FLEW OVER THE CUCKOO'S NEST (Raindog); HOWARD'S REVENGE, THE ALLBRIGHT FELLOW (Fifth Estate); THE THRIE ESTAITES (Edinburgh Festival Society); BROTHERS OF THUNDER, EUROPE, AWAY, FAITH HEALER (Traverse). Television includes: THE GOVAN GHOST STORY, TELL TALE HEARTS,SEEKER REAPER, TRUTH OR DARE (BBC); DR FINLAY, THE ADVOCATES, TAGGART (ITV). Film includes: BROND, THE SILENT SCREAM, BEING HUMAN, TRAINSPOTTING, BREAKING THE WAVE.

CHAHINE YAVROYAN *(Lighting Designer)*: Trained Bristol Old Vic School. Theatre work includes: THE TRIAL, METAMORPHOSIS, MISS JULIE, ZOO STORY, AGAMEMNON (London Theatre Group); NO.84 – NO.101 (People Show); MACBETH (Leicester Haymarket); USES OF ENCHANTMENT (ICA); THE LITTLE BLACK BOOK (The French Institute); GLORIA, I SURRENDER DEAR (The Place); HAUGHMOND DANCES (Haughmond Abbey); ASCENDING FIELDS (Fort Dunlop); ENNIO MARCHETTO (Hackney Empire); LA MUSICA DEUXIEMME, GAUCHO (Hampstead); HEDDA GABLER (Manchester Royal Exchange); HOUSE (Site Specific show in Salisbury); PYGMALION (Nottingham Playhouse); DARWIN'S FLOOD (Bush); 15 MINUTES TO 6 HOURS (Anatomy Dance Theatre); TANTAMOUNT ESPERANCE (Royal Court).

TRAVERSE THEATRE
THE COMPANY

* The Traverse Theatre has the support of the Pearson TV Theatre Writers' Scheme, sponsored by the Peggy Ramsay Foundation, administration by Pearson Television.

** This Theatre has the support of Scottish Television and the Calouste Gulbenkian Foundation under the Regional Theatre Young Director Scheme, administration by Channel Four Television.

TRAVERSE THEATRE
SPONSORSHIP

Sponsorship income enables the Traverse to commission and produce new plays and offer audiences a diverse and exciting programme of events throughout the year

We would like to thank the following companies for their support throughout the year

CORPORATE ASSOCIATE SCHEME

LEVEL ONE
Clydesdale Bank
Dundas & Wilson CS
Scottish Brewers
Scottish Equitable plc
Scottish Life Assurance Co
United Distillers

LEVEL TWO
Allingham & Co, Solicitors
Isle of Skye 8 Year Blend
NB Information
Mactaggart and Mickel Ltd
The Royal Bank of Scotland
Willis Corroon Scotland Ltd
Métier Recruitment

LEVEL THREE
Alistir Tait FGA Antique & Fine Jewellery, Gerrard & Medd Designers, KPMG, Scottish Post Office Board, Nicholas Groves Raines Architects, Moores Rowland Chartered Accountants

With thanks to Navy Blue Design, designers for the Traverse, and to George Stewarts the printers

The Traverse Theatre's work would not be possible without the support of:

THE SCOTTISH ARTS COUNCIL • EDINBVRGH •
THE CITY OF EDINBURGH COUNCIL

The Traverse receives financial assistance for its educational and development work from: Calouste Gulbenkian Foundation, Esmee Fairbairn Charitable Trust, The Peggy Ramsay Foundation, The Nancie Massey Charitable Trust

SHINING SOULS props, costumes and scenery built by Traverse workshops

Funded by the National Lottery

THE SCOTTISH ARTS COUNCIL
National Lottery Fund

Print Photography by Euan Myles
Production Photography by Sean Hudson
LEVER BROTHERS for Wardrobe Care

Registered Charity No.SCO 02368

ACT ONE

Scene One

ANN *enters as if she's come home from being out all night. She's in her early forties.*

ANN. Mandy! Are you up yet? – Mandy! It's six o clock in the morning! You've had plenty sleep (you've been asleep for nine year.)

She starts hunting out some candles. The candles have been used already and are stuck in saucers and a variety of household crockery. She lights the candles and marks out a space. Then she exits into the (presumed) interior of the house.

There's a silence. Then a strange yelp of fright, something which sounds almost not human. Then, more subdued, voices.

ANN re-enters with Tarot cards and waits inside the ring of candles. MANDY enters, wearing a white dressing-gown over pyjamas. This is ANN's twenty-year-old daughter.

MANDY. How's the bride?

ANN. Oh, y'know . . .

MANDY. What time is it?

ANN (*furious*). Oh for chrissake Mandy, what kinna question's that?

MANDY. What?

ANN. Just don't start me, OK? This is my wedding-day supposed to be, I've got enough terrors in my life without you and Time ganging up on me. It's about six.

MANDY Aw mammy.

ANN. *Yes* aw mammy! Six o clock already and I still haven't decided the least wee detail. And on top of everything else I'm alive.

Beat.

MANDY. I thought you were going to sleep here last night.

ANN. So I did! Then I got fed up and went round to Billy's.

MANDY. Which Billy's?

Beat.

ANN. Two's wrong. I should have learned that from my numerology. Three's harmony, two's confusion. Things get torn in two, two is how things start. Coming home from Billy's I thought, I've got two men in my life, I've got to choose, I've got to make a decision.

MANDY. And did you?

ANN. Yes.

MANDY. What decision did you make?

ANN. I decided to trust my woman's instincts.

MANDY. I see.

ANN. Should I?

MANDY. No.

ANN. No?

MANDY. It was your instincts that got you into this mess.

ANN. Oh god. – Please, Mandy, read my cards before it's too late: I'm in a situation that's goannae engulf me before I can do a thing about it.

MANDY. I can't.

ANN. What do ye mean you can't?

MANDY. I don't believe in the cards any more. I'm a Christian.

ANN. (You're the only one that's dark enough to read me.) You're a what?

MANDY. I'm a Christian.

ANN. You're cute as hell, I'll say that much. Give the cards a good shuffle, I don't want the same bad cards I always get.

MANDY. *You* have to shuffle. You're the seeker.

ANN. I'll jinx them.

MANDY. Shuffle the cards and ask them your question.

ANN *kneels beside the candles, shuffles, lays the cards down on the floor. Then* MANDY *joins her, lays out the first card.*

MANDY. The Two of Swords. There's two men in your life.

ANN. I know that! What have I to do?

MANDY. The woman is blindfold and holds a sword in each hand. You've a choice. But you don't trust yourself. Why should you, you're a mess – and if you can't trust yourself who can you trust.

MANDY *lays down the second card, across the first.*

The Moon. The Moon is Diana. The Moon is unfaithfulness. There's two men in your life and you're cheating on both of them. That's on one level. On another level it's worse than that. Everything in this world is a resemblance. Everything under the moon could be something else . . .

She lays down four cards one after another, each one as bad as the next.

ANN. Oh god. – Oh hell. – Oh my god. – Bloody hell.

The cards are so bad, ANN *can hardly look at them. She's shielding her eyes with her fingers.*

MANDY *wants to get her to look at them.*

MANDY. The cards are neither good or bad. The cards are a reflection. To understand the cards what you have to do is look for the pattern. What's the pattern? Look. Are you looking? What do you see? Can you see a pattern?

ANN. Let me look.

MANDY. What's the pattern?

ANN. I'm no sure . . .

MANDY. There's none. You asked me to blind you and I'm blinding you. The cards are a reflection. The cards are saying your past and your future your future and your past are going round in circles. You're uncreated, like when space was nothing but a dark wind and Time hadn't begun yet. You're a mess, without either –

ANN. Mandy!

MANDY. What?

ANN. Stop it! I'm. I've got Billy. Then I've got Billy. I'm. Mess? I'm. Mess? I'm. *Twiced!* I've said to Billy he can move in with me today . . .

MANDY. Which Billy?

ANN. . . . . I had to tell him *something*, to explain why I'm getting married to *Billy!*

MANDY. I see.

ANN (*quietly*). I'm guilty as hell.

MANDY. You keep making it worse.

ANN. I know that.

MANDY. You keep making it worse!

ANN. So do ye see my problem! – I know pills arenae the answer, Mandy, and the nurses have far nicer emergencies than me to clean up after (the wee angels) – but I mean it, Mandy (I feel

like shite-and-abortion as it is) so tell me something good's
going to happen or I'll go up to that wardrobe in the boys
bedroom with my pills and never come out again.

MANDY *lays out three more cards.*

MANDY. Let's look for the good then. Ignore The Devil: you're
in chains to the flesh but you know that already. And in looking
for the good what you've to remember is the cards are neither
good or bad. They're ambiguous.

ANN. Ambiguous?

MANDY. Two-faced. Like a lie. To make you look more deeply
beyond just what you can see. Look at all the twos you've got.
On one level you're being told you've got two chances. On a
higher level you're being told that the two must become one.
You've two men in your life and you only need one. – So. Are
you calmer now? You've too much dualism in your life. Will
we see what the outcome is?

ANN. Will it be good?

MANDY. The cards only reflect.

ANN. OK. Let's see.

MANDY *turns over the last card. They stare at it. It's The
Hanged Man. To* ANN *it's an image of despair.*

MANDY. The Hanged Man. – There's two ways to look at this
card. This is a card you have to look at twice.

MANDY *doesn't have the heart to go on.*

ANN *gets up.*

MANDY. I'll put out the candles.

ANN *exits.* MANDY *puts out the candles.*

Scene Two

A street. The same summer morning. CHARLIE *and* MAX *enter.
About two months ago* MAX *found* CHARLIE *crying in a pub and
took him back to his unfurnished flat. They share a flat, an
addiction to gambling and continuous cash-flow problems.*

It's early morning and this may affect their voice-levels.

CHARLIE. This is her.

MAX. Where?

CHARLIE. There.

MAX. Which one?

CHARLIE. That one. – I had a premonition of this. Walking down the road? Maybe no this. I'd a premonition of something. Walking down the road? I thought, either this is déjà vu or it's already happened, one of the two. – Have I done this before?

MAX. What?

CHARLIE. Have I came here to ask the former person I made my vows to to lend us some dinero?

MAX. Yeah.

CHARLIE. Yeah?

MAX. That's my recollection.

CHARLIE. What did I say to her?

MAX. You said we were skint some reason.

CHARLIE. I know we were skint, ya toxin. What reason did I say?

MAX. All I remember is you cried and she gave you some dosh.

CHARLIE. Because we don't want to repeat the same reason do we.

CHARLIE *gets a fag-packet out, lights a fag, puts the fagpacket back in his pocket.*

CHARLIE. Right. It's time she was up anyway. On you go, shout her up.

MAX. Give us a fag will ye.

CHARLIE. Naw.

MAX. Give us a fag till I wake up chrissake.

CHARLIE. I don't have any fags! We're skint, remember?

Beat.

MAX. I might be more in tune with myself in the mornings if you'd stop talking in your sleep.

CHARLIE. How, what do I say?

MAX. If you slept in another room.

CHARLIE. It's the floorboards.

MAX. What about them?

CHARLIE. I don't like them do I. They hurt my back.

MAX. That's good for it fuckssake. I sleep on the exact same floorboards you do, you don't hear me yelling for mercy. Get your thoughts in order before you go to sleep like I do and you'll sleep like a mummy. – Give us a fag will ye.

CHARLIE. How many generations do I have to listen to this!

MAX. I cannae wake up a near-stranger at half past seven on a Saturday morning unless I get some sustenance, can I. I'm doing you a favour here!

CHARLIE. Eh?

MAX. You blew my giro.

CHARLIE. I blew your giro?

MAX. Correct.

CHARLIE. You're steeped, Max.

MAX. Am I. You blew my giro on the dogs.

CHARLIE. I blew half your giro on the dogs. Which, you owed me from last week when you blew half my giro on the dogs.

MAX. I don't mind carrying ye, Charlie. I've been carrying ye ever since the night I met you bawling your eyes out in that pub and carried ye back to my flat. I'm no looking for plaudits. What I will say, it's no been easy. Now you want to borrow some dinero from your wife and you want me to shout her up at half past seven on a Saturday morning for the reason that if yir father-in-law saw you he'd chase ye with a hammer and tongs: I call that a favour, what do you call it? – She's your wife.

CHARLIE. Yes she's my wife, exactly she's my wife. Therefore it's my wife and therefore it's me that's to stand here and tell her a lot of lies, all so's we don't have to mug some seven-year-old for his fags that shouldnae be smoking in the first place so he's entitled to a good kicking and you're doing me a favour. Get honest with yourself.

Slight pause.

MAX. I don't know what I'm saying do I, I haven't had a fag yet. – So I just shout her name, get her to come out?

CHARLIE. Yeah.

MAX. What's her name again – Veronica?

CHARLIE. Margaret Mary.

MAX. I knew it was something papish. So I just shout her name, wake her up?

CHARLIE. And don't wake her da.

CHARLIE *stands aside.* MAX *stands under the window.*

MAX. Margaret Mary. – Margaret Mary. – Margaret Mary. – Nothing.

CHARLIE. Nothing?

MAX. The dozy pape's went and died in her sleep.

CHARLIE. Try it again.

MAX. You try. (Fuckn Romeo.)

CHARLIE. Try it a bit louder.

MAX. I don't want a whole nest of papes falling on top of my napper do I.

CHARLIE. Try it no too loud and no too quiet.

CHARLIE stands aside again.

MAX. Margaret Mary. – Margaret Mary.

CHARLIE. Nothing?

MAX. Dead.

CHARLIE. It's got to be getting on for – what ? -

MAX. – half seven, eight. The day's half gone, put it that way . . .

CHARLIE. Unreal.

MAX. . . . history.

CHARLIE. When is this country going to wake up? – Come on we'll go, I'll cry if I stay here.

As they start to go, MARGARET MARY *enters below in a nightie and dressing-gown.*

MARGARET MARY. Charlie.

CHARLIE. Margaret Mary. It's me.

MARGARET MARY. You'd better go. You've woke my da. What is it?

CHARLIE. I need to talk to you.

MARGARET MARY. I don't have any.

CHARLIE. It's no that.

MARGARET MARY. Last time I gave you money my da belted my ma in the jaw.

CHARLIE. Is that, is money the only thing we've got in common? I need – time.

MARGARET MARY. I've gave you years, Charlie. I don't understand you; one minute you're saying we're finished and you never want to see my ugly face again and the next you're back at my door crying your eyes out. – I can hear my da starting, I'd better go back in.

MARGARET MARY *starts to go back inside.*

CHARLIE. Margarita darlin! It's my mother. This is all so wrong but you asked me so I'm telling you. She's lying across at the Southern. She got taken very bad again through the night and – I didnae want to say this – apparently this is it.

MARGARET MARY. I don't know what to say to you, Charlie.

CHARLIE. Shock. – I *said*, I *said*: 'all I wanted was some time'. I got rushed into it. Nobody knows for sure when it actually happened but she got rushed to the Southern three or four in the morning.

MARGARET MARY. Oh god.

CHARLIE. So . . .

MARGARET MARY. Oh god.

CHARLIE. I've been up since five which explains what time it is. Time? Y'know?

MARGARET MARY. So how did you hear?

CHARLIE. My brother Vincent came round earlier on. He was very good, y'know? This is all wrong Margaret, I know that. My life's all wrong. At least I can say that now. At least I can see it. Whether I can retrieve the situation, that's another thing I don't know. Something like this happens you think about your cliché life. Y' know? What have I ever gave. Y' know? What have I ever gave. – So I came, just, thought you'd want to know. The day I married you my mammie was so proud of me. Then when we split up and I walked out on ye she told me I was rotten to the core and if she never saw me again it would be too soon. Which: she relented (thankfully). – She thought the world of you. – So. We're just going to jump a bus across to the Southern. (Dying, so we can see her any time.)

MARGARET MARY. Wait here. OK? I'll be back in a minute.

MARGARET MARY *goes inside. Long silence. Both* CHARLIE *and* MAX *are in tears.*

MAX. You OK?

CHARLIE. Eh?

MAX. OK?

CHARLIE. Yeah. I'm OK.

MAX. D'you think she believed you?

CHARLIE. I think so.

CHARLIE *gets his fag-packet out, lights a fag.*

CHARLIE. She's gone for her purse.

CHARLIE *takes a draw on his fag. Then he holds the fag out to* MAX.

Here.

MAX *stays where he is.*

MAX. Y're some man, you.

CHARLIE. Here.

MAX *crosses to* CHARLIE, *to accept the fag.*

MAX. Y're some man.

CHARLIE. I'm anointed.

Self-congratulation, yes, but he's disgusted with himself too.

MARGARET MARY *comes out with her purse.*

CHARLIE. Listen Margaret Mary pet, don't –

MARGARET MARY. Here. Here's a tenner.

CHARLIE. Right. What for?

MARGARET MARY. Just take it. You'll need something for taxis or something.

CHARLIE. Right. Don't if you haven't got it.

MARGARET MARY. Take it.

CHARLIE. Listen, thanks. Because I'm skint the now. So this is . . . can't think of the word . . . good.

MARGARET MARY. I better go in, Charlie. I'm in my dressing-gown. – The wee man misses ye. He keeps asking where his daddy is.

CHARLIE. How is the wee man?

MARGARET MARY. He misses ye. It's no so bad for me but he's no even three yet, it's hard for him to understand why you've gone. So I told him you were in the jail, I thought that would be the easiest. You should hear him. I say to him, 'Where's your daddy, John Paul?' And he goes, 'He's in the pokey!' Anyway. I better let you get on.

CHARLIE. I'll come round later, let you know how she is etcetera.

MARGARET MARY. Or even just phone me.

CHARLIE. Or phone. I'll phone you, phone you, phone will be better, for the both of us.

MARGARET MARY. I have to go.

CHARLIE *watches her go.*

CHARLIE. Margaret Mary.

MARGARET MARY *stops*.

CHARLIE. You know the worst of it? The worst thing is (stop
me if it gets too painful) the worst is I feel OK. Deep down it's
like – quiet. Earlier on, that was different again. Walking down
the road etcetera? No idea what I'm going to say to you or
(worst comes to worst) what my reactions will be. Jumps, head,
routines, somersaults. But now I'm standing here talking to
you, I feel good again. It's happened (my mammie I'm talking
about) or it's goannae happen or it might have even happened.
Maybe it's because of my Aunt Netty. She used to *make up*
people that had died in Canada or some place nobody was
going to check up on her so she could tell people the bad news.

MARGARET MARY. Charlie, you don't have to.

CHARLIE. I don't have to . . . ?

MARGARET MARY. You don't have to . . . explain.

CHARLIE. The point being (I know I don't have to) the point
being (I know I don't have to I want to) the point being (I've
lost my place). The point is my mammy's dying and so
painfulness or sad or whatever it is I'm feeling, anything I say
makes sense for once because I've got feelings again. Like,
when you're in love. And there's no more Time. Or death. Or
Time. – That's how I said Aunt Netty. Death made her feel
good too. – You go in, darlin'. You look cold.

MARGARET MARY *exits. Silence.* CHARLIE *puts the tenner
in his pocket.*

CHARLIE. Whereabouts round here do we get a paper? (I don't
even know what's got a card today.)

MAX. (Newmarket.)

CHARLIE. (Newmarket.) Eh?

MAX. Eh?

CHARLIE. Paper?

MAX. Might as well.

CHARLIE. I know that. I'm saying, where?

MAX. Did we pass a shop?

CHARLIE. Did we?

MAX. I think so. Yeah. Yeah I think we did.

CHARLIE. Right. Let's get away from here.

VINCENT *enters. He's a lot older than* CHARLIE. *He's
wearing a suit. He's done well for himself in life.*

VINCENT: Charlie?

CHARLIE. Vincent? How's my big brother? I just came round earlydoors to see if MM wanted a hand with the wee man. But she chased me, which, I can see her point of view too.

VINCENT (*disordered but not particularly fast*). No address so no way to contact you. So then yesterday, y'know? She got taken very bad again, rushed to hospital. She's had a bad night, Father Frank Saint Alphonsus got out of his bed to give her the Last Sacraments. She's doing good, the women are all saying she's done it before and come out the other end, but the doctor more or less gave me the nod that this was it.

CHARLIE. Slow down, Vincent. OK? Slow down. Who are we talking about here?

VINCENT: Yir mother.

CHARLIE. Right. Fine. You never said that.

VINCENT: I've got the car.

CHARLIE. Naw, Vincent. Naw. Don't get me wrong.

VINCENT: I'm going back there anyway.

CHARLIE. Vincent. Don't. OK? Don't.

VINCENT: I'm going back there anyway.

CHARLIE. Don't make me say something I'll regret. I hear a day after everyone else?

VINCENT: I explained.

CHARLIE. OK, forget it. It's done now. I need to go home (go to the hospital like this, are ye daft?). Change, get my thoughts (somersaults here) get my thoughts in order. OK?

VINCENT: She's Ward 22.

CHARLIE. Right. What hospital?

VINCENT: Sorry: brain, wrong, car, gears . . . She's across at the Vicky.

CHARLIE. Right. The Vicky did you say, or the Southern?

VINCENT: The Vicky.

CHARLIE. Right. I'll see you later, Vincent. I'll see you later on, eh? Whenever.

VINCENT: She's been asking for ye. You were her favourite, Charlie. You were her wee baby boy.

VINCENT *exits*.

CHARLIE. What's happening?

MAX. What's going on?

CHARLIE. That was a disgrace, that was.

MAX. What?

CHARLIE. Did ye see the suit he had.

MAX. That was a disgrace, that was. I'm sorry, Charlie, I know he's your brother but people like him get to me. People like him, it's all on the outside.

CHARLIE. That was an utter disgrace, that was. I hear a day after everyone else?

MAX. I don't even want to think about him, Charlie! – One thing anyway, you knew before he told you.

CHARLIE. Eh?

MAX. Yir mother. OK, you can call it coincidence –

CHARLIE. She's no been well has she.

MAX. So OK, in *that* sense (I'll retreat). But come on, Charlie: *you* get honest, *you* get honest. You didnae need Vincent to tell ye – you knew. Because she's your mother, that's how, because you're closer to her than your own skin. Likes of (when you were saying it to Margaret Mary?) . . . You were in tears, Charlie. You were in tears, son.

CHARLIE. She was in tears.

MAX. We were all in fuckn tears.

Beat.

CHARLIE. Right. I'll need to get myself a suit.

MAX. You want a suit?

CHARLIE. I cannae go and see my mammie like this, can I. I want her to see me the way I looked on my wedding-day. Y'know?

MAX. Listen, Charlie, don't say nothing more, OK? (Y'll offend me.) The suit's – understood. Understand?

CHARLIE. I want her to be proud of me, y'know.

MAX. Correct. – How much money have we got?

CHARLIE. I've got the tenner. How much you got?

MAX. I'm, penniless (as y'know). – Right. So!

CHARLIE. A tenner's a tenner.

MAX. We've got a tenner.

CHARLIE. We could go to The Barras.

MAX. We'll go to The Barras then.

CHARLIE. Pick up something cheap.

MAX. Correct.

CHARLIE. We better get you some fags, eh son? – Right then. Fags suit and we'll be brand new. OK, Max?

MAX. OK, Charlie.

CHARLIE. OK, son? Then we can go across to the Southern Vicky wi a bit of dignity and a bunch of flowers and see her proud.

MAX. You're going to be fine, Charlie son, I'll watch out for ye, son. So long as you exercise a wee bit caution, you'll be fine. A day like today: these are the kinna days ye have to watch. These are the days that can tempt ye. I've come across these kinna days before, you have to watch and no get carried away with your emotions.

CHARLIE *nods and goes.*

It's hard, I know that.

CHARLIE'*s gone.*

But ye cannae get carried away with a tenner.

MAX *goes.*

Scene Three

The same street, later on. ANN *and* MANDY *enter. They've been shopping and* MANDY'*s holding a bride's wedding-bouquet.*

MANDY. Where are you going? *We* live *here.*

ANN. Oh! So we do.

ANN, *who's blindly walked past where she lives, stops. She goes back a step or two towards the house, then stops again.*

MANDY. What time's Billy coming?

ANN. Which Billy?

MANDY. Either.

ANN. I forget what times I told them. Anyway, you know what like they are, they'll both be early. I suppose I should count my blessings. Most women would be happy with just the one lovely man . . .

MANDY. Are ye coming in?

ANN. Or could we maybe just . . .

MANDY. Just?

ANN. . . . escape . . .

> BILLY 1 *enters. He's carrying one of those metal cases hireshops give you suits in and some flowers.*

BILLY 1. Ann.

ANN. Billy.

BILLY 1. I got you some flowers.

ANN. Oh Billy. You shouldn't've.

BILLY 1. Ahch, I wake up on my wedding-day to find it's the most gorgeous day in the history of the universe since the effn rainbow? – I'd no choice. Did you sleep?

ANN. Where?

BILLY 1. Last night?

ANN. Uh huh.

BILLY 1. I lay in my bed sat up lay in my bed sat up lay in my bed sat up. Then I heard the first bus.

ANN. I got a coupla hours.

BILLY 1. Nervous?

ANN. Kind of.

BILLY 1. All last night I stayed awake thinking am I sure, am I absolutely sure? Have I got enough love in me to last thirty forty years? And the truth is, Ann, who am I kidding? I'm in chains to you like the seas in chains to the moon. If I'm an ocean you're its heart. Wherever you want to go, I'll race you.

ANN. Billy, I told Billy I'd 'speak' to you. I'm telling you that to let you know. I'm no saying I will 'speak' to ye, I'm just telling you what I told Billy.

BILLY 1. When were you talking to Billy?

ANN. Oh Billy darlin'. I had a sentence about it but it's gone.

MANDY. Here comes Billy 2.

BILLY 1. Make up another sentence quick then!

ANN. I wish other women had my problems.

BILLY 1. Ann –

> BILLY 2 *enters, carrying three suitcases and some flowers.*

BILLY 2. Ann.

ANN. Billy!

BILLY 2. I brought you some flowers.

ANN. Oh Billy!

BILLY 1. I like the suitcases, Billy. Don't not come back and visit now and again.

BILLY 2. How, where am I going?

BILLY 1. You tell me.

BILLY 2. Have you *spoken* to him yet?

ANN. I *said*.

BILLY 2. You *said?*

ANN. I have to 'speak' to you too, Billy.

BILLY 2. Don't go back on me now, Ann. After last night?

ANN. Shhh, I know.

BILLY 1. 'Last night'? Who's he talking to, Ann?

BILLY 2. The plans we made. How it would be. Even the en suite shower in the bedroom I promised to build. – We were made for each other, Ann. I know I cannae, like, talk, Ann. And OK Ann, I don't have a vocabulary or even just ordinary words so you'll have to make do or make up your own but I love you so many different ways a day an hour my heart brain can't keep up.

ANN *crosses to* BILLY 2.

ANN. Oh Billy! See last night? I don't pretend to understand it or even remember what happened. It was the night before I made my wedding vows wasn't it. One minute I was lying in my bed reflecting on the vows I was going to make and the next I was ringing your bell. I suppose my instincts were telling me to panic so I fled the house and ran to you –

BILLY 2. – where you always run.

ANN. – where I always run.

BILLY 2 *gives her his flowers.*

BILLY 1. I feel sadness more than anything. He's no listening to ye, Ann. He's no listening to what you're *not* saying.

BILLY 2. If you give me your keys Ann I'll let myself in, while you –

ANN. – while I – ?

BILLY 2. – while you Billy.

ANN *comes back to get the keys out of her handbag.*

BILLY 1. Is he deaf, what's she just told you Billy, what're you just after telling him Ann? Open your eyes, Billy, she said no!

ANN. Mandy, will you hold my flowers while I get into my bag to get my keys?

MANDY *doesn't take the flowers.*

MANDY. Oh look: everybody's watching us from their windows. Even the black alsatian that baby-sits for the four-year-old across the street is watching. The four-year-old's probably away making the toast.

ANN. Will you hold my flowers, Mandy,

BILLY 1. See last night, Billy: how did you interpret it.

BILLY 2. How did I interpret it? I took it, me and Ann's lying in bed . . .

BILLY 1 (*hurrying* BILLY 2). . . . . right, fine, right . . .

BILLY 2. . . . . making plans together . . .

BILLY 1. . . . . fine, right, fine . . .

BILLY 2. . . . . lying in bed making plans . . . how much detail do ye want, Billy? I took it, she'd came running to me the night before she called off her wedding.

BILLY 1. You took it wrong then, as I suspected. Face it, Billy. She was being polite. She was seeing you one last time wasn't she. She's too effn nice, that's her problem.

BILLY 2. It's all down to interpretation isn't it, you take it one way I take it another. I listen to what Ann says, you listen to what she doesnae say.

BILLY 1. See last night, Ann?

ANN. Don't expect me to feel guilty, Billy, you're the one that's got some explaining to do. If you're that worried about marrying me you stay awake all night then no *wonder* I've got my doubts.

MANDY. Oh, there's the four-year-old now – standing on a chair up at the window – wave!

MANDY *takes the flowers from* ANN.

MANDY. Aw, I thought she was waving. She's just kinna wiping the window with her toast.

BILLY 1. See last night? You only hurt yourself, beautiful. Like you always do. Ever since the day I held you close on the couch and you told me your life and I understood, you knew it was me and you and no one else for ever. And you being you (and what with the two tragedies you've had in your life) you had to make things hard for yourself. Then Billy comes along and he's the perfect obstacle. I mean, I happen to think you've got enough depressants in your life without Billy but I understand. I even understand last night, that's how I can be so stupid (philosophical about it). Because I know how badly you must be hurting.

BILLY 1 *gives* ANN *his flowers. She takes them. There's a pause.*

ANN. Don't make it harder for me then.

BILLY 1. I'm trying to make it easier, Ann.

ANN. That's what's making it harder, Billy.

BILLY 1 (*fearing the worst*). What're you saying to me, Ann.

ANN. I wish I could start again Billy but I can't, I wish I could take my ugly face off and start all over again Billy but I can't, and meantime Billy, meantime, I don't like ye *looking* at me the way you look at me.

ANN's *crying.*

BILLY 2. She's crying Billy, *chrissake!*

BILLY 1. Yeah Billy, you're perched there like a sad omen. She's waiting on you to take the hint and fly away.

BILLY 2. Will you give me the keys Ann, because the quicker I get inside the quicker I don't have to punch someone.

BILLY 1. That's the difference between me and you: violence.

BILLY 2. So give me the heart keys seizure now Ann!

BILLY 1. Ann, are you going to explain violence to him!

MANDY. Violence? You said that was the difference.

ANN, *not wanting to get sandwiched between the two* BILLYS, *moves forward out of the firing line.*

BILLY 1. It's your decision, Ann.

BILLY 2. She's made her decision, Billy.

ANN. Billy – I've said the same words to the both of you, Billy. I've said 'I love you' to him too Billy. I can't trust myself to open my mouth any more. I've decided I can't go on; I've decided I can't make a decision; I've decided I can't nothing, no until I get a new (I'm only being practical) a new (I'm only being realistic) a new big (space to hang in).

Pause.

BILLY 2. Is it a big wardrobe you mean?

ANN *turns away from him.*

Is it a big wardrobe she means?

MANDY *turns away from him.*

Is the one in the boys' bedroom no big enough? I mean, if it was big enough for the two boys . . .

ANN (*fierce, warning*). Billy!

BILLY 1. Billy. Back off.

BILLY 2. I can understand you no wanting to use it right enough, given the, given the, given the (throat's dried). – You can keep it to hang *me* in, Ann. Eh Ann? You can keep it to hang *me* in.

Beat. ANN *moves towards the house.*

ANN. I better put these flowers in a vase.

BILLY 2. We could pick up a good-size wardrobe at The Barras. Ann, wardrobes coming out the walls there.

ANN. It'll take the both of ye to carry it,

BILLY 1. If that's what you want, Ann.

ANN. OK.

BILLY 2. And then will you make a decision, Ann.

ANN. Yes.

ANN *exits. The two* BILLYS *collect their stuff.*

MANDY. Listen, seen as how this is the only decision you're going to hear all day, I thought I'd better let you know I've decided that today's the day, OK? She's hardly looked the road I walk on for nine year. Today's the day she's going to look me in the face .

MANDY *exits after* ANN.

BILLY 2. Sphinx? Is that the word for it?

BILLY 1. Word for what?

BILLY 2. She's gave us a task hasn't she.

BILLY 1. What chance have you got, Billy son. She's no even testing you. She's testing me. You can come to the Barras if you want son, help me cart the wardrobe back. You'll be carrying your own coffin.

The BILLYS *exit in the direction of the house.*

Scene Four

The next four scenes are set in The Barras: a market-place which spreads out over several streets, lanes, buildings and yards.

In this scene we're in a space behind a street of stalls. We see the back of the stalls, so maybe we see the backs of two or three stall-holders and hear their spiels.

NANETTE *enters carrying a soapbox, followed by* PROPHET JOHN. PROPHET JOHN *has an antagonistic relationship with himself, the world and with his own gift of prophecy. His energy is, in the true sense of the word, daemonic. When the spirit is upon*

*him he is very powerful; but at all other times he is extremely bad-
tempered and irritable. There's an anger in him he tries to contain
but can't.*

NANETTE *puts down the soapbox, gets out a flask from her bag.*

NANETTE. D'you want some soup?

PROPHET JOHN. What kind of soup.

NANETTE. Some soup I made.

PROPHET JOHN. 'Some soup I made.'

NANETTE. D'you want some?

> *Beat.*

PROPHET JOHN. No.

NANETTE. No?

PROPHET JOHN. No!

NANETTE. It's good home-made soup.

PROPHET JOHN. No thank you.

NANETTE. Are you no hungry?

> *No reply.*
>
> Eh? Are you no hungry, John?
>
> *She holds out a cup of soup.*
>
> Here. – Here.

PROPHET JOHN. Nanette, will you stop please murdering me.

NANETTE. Eh?

PROPHET JOHN. 'Eh?'

NANETTE. Cheesey peeps!

PROPHET JOHN. I've indicated that I don't wish to be a part of
your soup. Don't keep on keeping on.

NANETTE. There's no need for language.

PROPHET JOHN. What language did I use?

NANETTE (*avoiding*). Anyway!

PROPHET JOHN. What bad language did I use?

NANETTE. What about here? You'll get a good crowd here.
There's plenty people come to the Barras on a Saturday. I'll
stay and help build your crowd but then I'll have to get back
and mind my stall. – Eh? What about here?

PROPHET JOHN. I've got nothing to say.

NANETTE. The spirit will speak. – Eh?

PROPHET JOHN. No! – Nobody listens to me.

NANETTE. Och, away ye go! You 'speak' to plenty people. You 'speak' to a right good few of us. When the spirit takes you you're like to Noah's dove. There's plenty that won't listen I'm no saying that, and there's plenty that listen but don't hear I'm no saying that. They can't hear the words of the spirit unless the spirit opens their ears can they. – Eh?

PROPHET JOHN. I've been struck dumb. – The spirit. The spirit's like a lion in the land. He's roaming the land looking for prey. He wants the flesh from my bones. He wants the air from my lungs. He wants the tongue from my head. Then he'll stand up in my bare bones and prophesy. – Who am I? Am I a prophet like Ezekiel? Or Isaiah? Or Jeremiah? Or Amos? Or Zechariah? Or Habbakuk? Or Hosea? Or Daniel? Or Malachi?

PROPHET JOHN *is now, in spite of himself, in the possession of his daemon – and at this point* ANN *and* MANDY *enter, followed by the two* BILLYS.

I went to Death and said 'Where do I go to find Wisdom?' And Death said, Death said 'I don't know!' 'I don't know,' Death said, 'I only hear rumours of her.' – Yes! Yes! Yes, Israel, yes I'm a prophet! Your prophets, Israel, are like ruin-haunting jackals. Don't come too close – better to stand at the outskirts of the camp and listen to the jackals barking in the distant ruins. Why have you come here? What is it you want?

BILLY 1. Ann, we'll go take a look at –

BILLY 2. – take a look at wardrobes Ann.

BILLY 1. Are you coming, Ann?

PROPHET JOHN. 'Does a girl forget her ornaments, does a bride forget her wedding-wreath? Then why have you forgotten me?'

ANN. You two go on.

The BILLYS *exit.*

PROPHET JOHN. 'Does a woman forget her jewellery or a bride her wedding-sash? Yet you have forgotten me days without number.'

CHARLIE *and* MAX *enter.* MAX *opens a fresh cigarette-pack, puts two fags in his mouth, lights them, inhales. Then he opens his paper and studies the racing form (and that's him happy for the rest of the scene.)* CHARLIE *watches and listens.*

PROPHET JOHN. Once there was a woman. – Yes, Israel! Yes! Revile me! Denigrate me! Heap abuse upon my head! Is it me that says this? – no! – Once there was a woman in the land of Israel. One night she was lying with her husband in their tent and she heard Yahweh God of Israel speak to her saying, 'Does a girl forget her ornaments or a bride her wedding-wreath? Then why have you forgotten me?' And she listened to Yahweh

God of Israel and left me sleeping in the tent and stole away. When I arose that morning he could smell her perfume on our sheets, the scent of cinnabar on our pillow; and I waited for her day and night and night and day. I looked for her on the road-sides and sought her out in the cities; as well in the temple as in the jackal-haunted ruins; and everywhere I went I shouted, 'Does a woman forget her jewellery or a bride her wedding-wreath? Then how come you've forgotten me?'

ANN (*to* NANETTE). Is he speaking to me?

NANETTE. When the spirit descends the spirit descends.

PROPHET JOHN *takes his coat off and approaches closer to* ANN.

PROPHET JOHN. 'Does a girl forget her ornaments or a bride her wedding-sash? Yet you have forgotten me days without number.'

He throws his coat over her head – and holds her strongly by the arms. He does this with authority and power.

CHARLIE *and* MANDY *look on, concerned, but held back from interfering by the sense that some power is present and no way of knowing whether the power is violent or healing.*

PROPHET JOHN (*to* ANN). There is a lion in the land. He wants the breath from your body. He wants the flesh from your haunches. He wants the bones you stand up in. After he's eaten he'll fall asleep.

PROPHET JOHN *embraces* ANN *strongly. She seems to yield to this. But to* CHARLIE *the embrace is becoming uncomfortably strong – like the embrace of a lion – and* CHARLIE *decides to intervene.*

CHARLIE. Haw! You! Enough! Down! Drop it! Leave! Back! Back!

PROPHET JOHN *lets go of* ANN *and backs away to a safer distance.*

Now CHARLIE *is beside* ANN *and holds her, to calm her. But* ANN *wants to get the coat off her head and is distressed and doesn't want to be touched.*

CHARLIE. It's OK, it's OK, it's OK, it's OK.

He gets the coat off her head.

ANN. Who are you?

CHARLIE. I'm –

ANN feels very naked and needs to hide herself somehow; with her hands, with words; while she sorts herself out.

ANN. I'm OK, it's OK, I'm OK, I'm fine, I'll be fine.

CHARLIE. Are you sure?

ANN. I'm OK, it's OK, I'm all, I'll be fine, I'm fine, I'm all outside in.

CHARLIE. He was kind of mauling you there.

ANN. I don't know how it happened, he kind of (it's my own fault, I let him!) he kinna undid me.

PROPHET JOHN. The lion stands over his prey.

CHARLIE. Back!

PROPHET JOHN (*a bit on the back foot, wary*). Is there no god in Israel that you have to go and consult oracles? Is there no god in Israel that you go and consult Beel-Zebub, god of Ekron; or the goddess-whore of Babylon. I fed you full and you became adulterers, well-fed roving stallions, each one neighing for his neighbour's wife. And because you have broken your covenant with me the Lord your God who is a jealous god, I am coming to trample you underfoot in the valley of Jezreel and raise you up as a cloud of dust.

CHARLIE. (See people that shout) I can shout at people too you know! I'm going to hunt you, my friend, you're everything that's all wrong the modern world: where's your structure (ya ugly big ride ye) where's your shape? (You're like a burst bin-bag) can you no keep anything in? Eh? Can you not keep nothing in? Does the word 'pish' mean nothing to you? Because it's about time you took a few lessons from a three-year-old and delineated a few lines! You're you, I'm me; this is outside, you should be inside; put your rubbish inside a binbag and then outside in the bin – and don't spill it all over the streets (I don't want to slip on your leftovers do I). I've got enough going on in my jumps, somersaults, suit, head without having to intermingle my thoughts with yours. So g'on! Away home to the bedsit; away home and cry in the wilderness; away home and listen to yourself!

CHARLIE *uses this speech to drive* PROPHET JOHN *and* NANETTE *from the stage. He also uses* PROPHET JOHN's *coat. He completes this expulsion by throwing* PROPHET JOHN's *coat after him. It's a job well done.*

CHARLIE (*fast, straight, without a pause*). I applaud a man like that, who is he? Some people would condemn the man but no way no way no way I agree with him: if he's saying everything's all wrong the modern world then yes, correct, everything is all wrong, (him included.) Are you OK?

ANN. Yes. I don't know how I get myself into these things, I don't seem to have any self-control.

CHARLIE. What is it you're looking for?

ANN. I wish I knew!

CHARLIE. You must be looking for something.

CHARLIE *indicates the Barras.*

ANN. Aw, you mean, what am I looking for? I thought you meant what am I looking for?

CHARLIE. I'm looking for a suit. I like to wear a suit, even just no for anything special, y'know: I'm too old-fashioned, that's my problem. For the reason the old dear's a hunner and something (seventy odds). Sad. Y'know? So! Don't make me a stranger next time, what's your name again?

ANN. Me? Emm, Ann.

CHARLIE *offers his hand and they shake.*

CHARLIE. Charlie. Don't make me a stranger, Ann. – And who's this? Are you two related in any way? Because she's lovely enough to be your sister.

ANN. Mmmm, she's my gaughter.

CHARLIE. She's your what?

MANDY. I'm her gaughter. Gandhi.

CHARLIE. It's a pleasure to meet you, Mahatma. You see and keep your mammie out of trouble. – Well, if it was another day. But today (to draw a line) today's a day to get the head down and graft away and if it breaks my heart that's all to the good. – OK, Max?

MAX *is still reading The Sporting Life and working out accumulators.*

Max, are you coming? Suit Max suit – c'mawn, c'mawn, cmawwwwn – look at the state of him – look at the state of ye, Max – because see life, Max, you can not-live life all you want but you can't not-live death.

And with that bon mot, CHARLIE *exits, followed by* MAX. ANN *checks off-stage to see where he's gone to.*

ANN. Where has he been all my life!

MANDY. Did you think he was good-looking?

ANN. I wouldnae say he was good-looking. But he was so sad and so complicated and so dignified and so decisive and so (I donno) so handsome.

MANDY. He seemed quite keen.

ANN. D'you think so?

MANDY. Yeah. He was quite keen on you too for a bit but he kinna lost interest.

ANN. D'you think so?

MANDY. Mmmm.

ANN. What makes you think that?

MANDY. Aw c'mon, I don't want to say it: it's no very nice.
OK: let's just say there's a lot less to you than meets the eye. I
mean, you don't even have a character. It's like, 'Who are ye?'
I mean, a man shows the least interest in you and your wee
heart's panicking like a flock of pigeons, or like you're goannae
die in the next two minutes.

ANN is dumbstruck for a moment.

ANN. Are you looking for a fight?

MANDY. Maybe.

ANN. 'Maybe.'

ANN starts to walk towards the same exit CHARLIE exited.

MANDY. Where are you going?

ANN. I'm just going to see if Charlie needs any help choosing a
suit.

MANDY. OK. I just think he kinna lost interest in ye.

BILLY 2 enters.

BILLY 2. We've seen a good-sized wardrobe, Ann, if you'd like to
come and see it.

ANN (*furious*). I'll be right there, Billy, stop nagging me, will ye,
you've been biting my ear all bloody day!

BILLY 2. It's a good size, I'll say that. It's just round the corner,
Ann, so: whenever.

ANN (*shouting*). OK, Billy, I'm coming!

BILLY 2 goes.

MANDY. I'll see you later on, OK?

ANN. Why, where are you going?

MANDY. Nowhere. – Do you think sex and violence are
different?

ANN. Eh?

MANDY. I think they can both be an end in themselves.

ANN. You're no too old for a slap on the tits milady.

MANDY. So you agree then. – I'll let you get on, you'd better go
and Billy.

ANN. Mandy! Will you get back here !

MANDY's *exited in the same direction as* CHARLIE.

Oh for goodness sake, Mandy, you're more shallow than a bloody – mirror! Right. I see. That's the way it's to be, is it. We're going to tear each other's faces off all day and see who's the ugliest?

ANN *goes off in the direction of the* BILLYS.

Good grief. All I want is one happy day.

Scene Five

Interior. Racks of second-hand suits. The perimeter is lined with pairs of second-hand shoes. CHARLIE *and* MAX *enter.*

CHARLIE. Suits.

MAX. Quiet in here.

CHARLIE. Shoes an' all.

MAX. You want shoes an' all?

CHARLIE. I'm just indicating the shoes.

MAX. You want to try some on?

CHARLIE. Naw.

MAX. Naw.

CHARLIE. Shoes are a man's character. You don't get that second-hand do ye.

   CHARLIE *approaches the suit-rack. He doesn't touch the suits, just looks at them.*

MAX. The dead . . . The dead have no taste have they. – Why do I want to clear my throat in here? What do I want to keep out? What do I want to expel? – I'm a wee bit concerned getting, Charlie. You're too vulnerable, Charlie. You're too wide open.

   CHARLIE *goes round to the other side of the suit-rack from* MAX. *They can't see each other.*

MAX. D'you see a suit you like?

   MANDY *enters unseen.*

MAX. Charlie? D'you see a suit you like? – I've seen days like this happen before. Some days it's like the day's out to hunt ye. So beware, Charlie. Suit, I respect that. But I see a man that lives more invisible than that, more private. Like your voice, Charlie. Your voice, Charlie . . . is like a secret that you're keeping even from yourself.

CHARLIE *touches the sleeve of one of the suits, lets it go.*

CHARLIE. Let's get out of here.

MAX. You don't want a suit?

CHARLIE. I want to visit my mammie in a suit someone hasnae got old and died in a coupla times.

MAX. You want a new suit?

CHARLIE. Correct.

MAX. Correct. – How much money we got?

CHARLIE. A fiver . . . odds.

MAX. You need to eat, Charlie. This is the unfortunate thing. Certain things, Charlie, whether we like them or no . . . money, Charlie, or . . . hunger. I know I'm hungry. I'm dizzy getting. Can I suggest something? Can I suggest we've reached an impasse? – Charlie? Can I suggest we've reached an impasse?

CHARLIE. Yeah.

MAX. Good. So therefore can I suggest (see if this gets us any further forward) can I suggest we get ourselves something to eat then go to the bookie's? – (see if that gets us any further forward).

CHARLIE. Put on an accumulator?

MAX. Correct.

CHARLIE (*straight*). I've a bad feeling, Max. I've a bad bad feeling, Max. I'm no sure my mammie's goannae wait till the fourth favourite comes in at Newmarket, Max, y'know. That's my feeling.

MAX. Charlie (fuckssake, Charlie). Are you OK?

CHARLIE. I've a bad sick feeling, Max. Y'know? How bad it is I don't know. It's bad enough.

MANDY. Do you need any help?

MAX. Naw.

MANDY. Jesus says Follow me. Follow me and I'll save you. I'll lead you out of the darkness and into the light. I'm a Christian.

MAX. Charlie?

CHARLIE *appears from round the other side of the suit-rack.*

MANDY. Hiya, it's me. I've come to save ye.

CHARLIE. Good enough. You got any money?

MANDY. Eh?

CHARLIE *produces a fiver.*

CHARLIE. Look: fiver: is this on its own or have you got a mate for it?

MANDY. Is this a trick?

CHARLIE. Yes. So back off.

MANDY produces a fiver.

MANDY. There. Now what?

CHARLIE. This is a lighter. See? What you do is wrap the fiver round your wrist then burn a hole through it.

MANDY. Why?

MAX. Because ye cannae do it, that's why.

CHARLIE. Impossible.

MAX. Can't be done.

MANDY. I see. What's the point then?

CHARLIE. Watch. I've got a fiver you've got a fiver. I give you my last lonely fiver which is the only company I've got in the entire world, OK? Now you give me your fiver.

MANDY. OK.

They exchange fivers.

CHARLIE. Thanks, Gandhi: you're a Christian. So now you've got my one and only last fiver even though that leaves me with fuck-all fuck-all and my insides like a half-full can of lager the morning after a party that someone's used for an ashtray. – You burn a wee hole through that fiver onto your wrist you keep it. That's the bet. You fail to burn a hole through it I get my fiver back.

MANDY. I don't like pain. Why don't you try it?

CHARLIE. You're offering the bet to me?

MANDY. Yeah.

CHARLIE. OK, give me my fiver then.

MANDY. You can use the fiver of mine you've got.

Beat.

CHARLIE. You're offering the bet to me?

MANDY. Yeah.

CHARLIE. OK. I accept.

MANDY. Is there a trick?

CHARLIE. Are you giving the bet to me?

MANDY. Yeah.

CHARLIE. Sure?

MANDY. Yeah.

CHARLIE. Good. Yes there's a trick.

MAX. Caveat emptor.

CHARLIE. Have you seen boiling chipfat? (So I can teach you.)

MANDY. In the chippie.

CHARLIE. That's the trick: agony. The chippie, the chipfat spits
up at him he can accept that. But he doesn't stand there and
pour the chipfat over his wrists does he. So that's the question.
How much *pain* can I endure? How much *pain* can I inflict
upon myself? How much pain can I endure to inflict upon
myself? OK, Christian?

MANDY. Yeah, that sounds like it might be quite good.

   CHARLIE *lights his lighter*.

CHARLIE. OK, Max?

   MAX *comes across and holds the fiver against* CHARLIE'*s*
   wrist. MANDY *finds a good place to watch the trick from.*

CHARLIE. OK, Christian? You watching?

   In the dim interior light CHARLIE *holds the lit lighter to his*
   face.

CHARLIE. OK, Max?

MAX. I'm OK, you OK?

CHARLIE. I've got a bad bad feeling, Max. – I want to take this
slow. OK? I want to approach the pain.

   Slowly CHARLIE *brings the lighter to his wrist and holds it*
   there. It's painful.

MANDY. Is it hurting yet?

   CHARLIE *can't bear the pain.*

CHARLIE. OK, that's it, I'm no doing it. OK, Christian? Give me
my fiver back (I'm only being honest with ye) give me my fiver
back or I'll cut your eyes open.

MAX. You'd better do as he tells you, gorgeous.

CHARLIE. You'd better do as he tells you, gorgeous, because I
am not a well man suddenly and my insides being empty
there's no much to stop me from slapping you about the place.
Bad? You don't know how bad badness can be, so don't fanny
me around because I don't have the time!

MAX. You're in grave danger, darling.

CHARLIE. Because how no well I am (I've no been living good, have I) and how no well I am I'm waiting for a sign from God – that's (only fair) let you know the danger you're in.

In the face of this storm of violence MANDY *is reasonably serene.*

MANDY. You lost the bet. You owe me a fiver.

CHARLIE. Can someone translate her for me? I'm lost.

MANDY. I bet you're the type that mugs wee seven-year-olds for their fag-money. Are ye?

MAX. Right, you: fuck off while we're still being pleasant.

MANDY. Not until you give me my fiver.

MAX. Is she on drugs?

CHARLIE. Give her the fiver ya diddy.

MAX. Eh?

CHARLIE. You're standing there like a miserable wet shiteyarsed sheep bleating in the rain.

MAX. Am I.

CHARLIE. Give her the fiver, ya grass-muncher.

MAX *hands over the fiver.*

MAX. I'm losing the plot here, Charlie.

MANDY. So. Do you see my Christian breastplate of faith? Do you see how unscathed it is?

CHARLIE. I'm stood here admiring ye.

MANDY. Good. I'm glad.

CHARLIE. 'God.' (You're gorgeous, by the way.)

MANDY. Am I?

CHARLIE. 'God.' OK, I can accept that. Because I give up. I'm beat. I'm nothing. I'm a bad bad feeling. And likes of with my mammie across at the Vicky dying . . . Y'know? So shirt shoes and a suit someone hasnae died in a coupla times, I can prepare myself, away across to the Vicky and break my heart. Obviously.

MANDY. And you want help?

CHARLIE. I apologise for raising my voice back there. I'm too complex, that's my problem. I do things (wrong!) – things do things (even that's no quite true).

MANDY. And you want help?

CHARLIE. Listen: I'm sorry. Right? Yeah.

CHARLIE *thinks she's going to give him the two fivers now and holds out his hand.* MANDY *just looks at him.*

MANDY. You're in a bad way aren't ye. It's like you're too many, or it's like you're too open, y'know?, like the river or something and you've got infested with the dead bodies and then you open your mouth and they all come pouring out. I hope you don't mind me saying that.

CHARLIE. No. I . . .

MANDY. I'm just shining a light. It might take you a while to get used to it seen as how you've been in the dark so long.

CHARLIE. . . . no, I think I see what you're hinting at.

MANDY. OK, you can come with me then.

MANDY *starts to exit.*

CHARLIE. Where to?

MANDY. I'll take you home with me if you want. We've got loads of mens clothes – so bath, shirt, shoes, a couple of suits, and you can go and see your mammie looking brand new. OK?

CHARLIE. That would be – very kind of ye.

MANDY. OK then. Follow me.

MANDY *exits.* CHARLIE *and* MAX *make a move in the same direction.*

MAX. Charlie. I'm no goannae ask you what's happening because whatever it is it's not food mouth stomach: but see the art of conmanship, Charlie: the art of conmanship, Charlie, is to con the other person. Otherwise you're Santa Claus ya cunt.

CHARLIE. I got carried away with the truth didn't I. I'd no idea what I was saying.

CHARLIE *exits in same direction as* MANDY.

MAX. Charlie, if I don't eat shortly I'm goannae have to hurt somebody. I'm goannae have to eat somebody. – Charlie? – Charlie?

MAX *exits in the same direction as* CHARLIE.

Scene Six

Exterior, the Barras. MANDY *enters followed by* CHARLIE. MAX *traipses on after them.*

CHARLIE. It's good of you to do this for me, Christian. Do you do this a lot?

MANDY. No.

CHARLIE. I mean, I acknowledge your goodness taking me into the bosom of your family. Will your ma be there too?

MANDY. Why d'you ask that?

MAX. Can we pause here Charlie to (take stock) break her arm, Charlie? Charlie, can we pause here to take stock? Because we've passed the hot dogs.

MANDY. Eh? Why d'you ask that?

CHARLIE. It's just the way my somersaults, jumps, double-back mind works. I'm no trying to exclude your ma (she's lovely too). I'm concerned what she might say.

MANDY. I'll just tell her I'm trying to save ye.

MAX. I'm running out of excuses for ye, Charlie. Your mother can only last so long (the truth, Charlie), your mother's only an excuse for so long!

MANDY. Do you ever think 'I'm alive!'?

CHARLIE. I am alive.

MANDY. But do you never, like, think 'I'm alive!' and, like, you're so happy you want to tear your scalp off.

CHARLIE. Listen, life's no a good subject for me the now.

MANDY. If I was a tree, like, in the country (we got sent to a home there once), if I was a tree, like, in the country and I was, like, really tall and it was, like, a really nice sunny day, I'd be so happy I'd topple over. I wouldn't be able to stand up.

CHARLIE. You're an angel, you are.

MANDY. Don't worry: I'm not as good as I look.

CHARLIE. You're giving me hope. – To be honest with you, Mandy: I haven't been living good. Time. Y'know? You marry, have a kid, leave them. Then you think, did I do that? Then, once upon a time, there was the cherubim, seraphim, thrones, dominions, powers; virtues, principalities; archangels, angels. Nice. Y'know?

The two BILLYS *enter carrying a huge big fucker of a wardrobe, followed by* ANN. *We see them as if in long-shot. An image accompanied by music.* MANDY *sees this and wants to exit.*

MANDY. Anyway. Let's get going.

MAX. Charlie, have you forsaken leave of your senses? Are you going to let her wander off with your cash?

CHARLIE *turns round to talk to* MAX – *sees the vision.*

CHARLIE. Max, why don't you – . – Look at that. Look at that, Mandy.

MANDY. Oh uh huh.

CHARLIE. How do you interpret that? Two men walk behind a woman carrying a coffer. The woman's wearing black. So right away we're talking about Fate, yeah? I look at that and I want to know the whole sad story. Who's she? Who are they? What have they done to make her so unhappy? She looks so sad and so womanly and so longing . . .

MANDY. I sometimes think men should be blinded at birth. I don't mean that to be horrible, their mothers could do it.

MAX. Blind would be fine by me.

MANDY. So they learned how to not look.

MAX. Blind me so long as she put something in my blind deluded mouth.

ANN *turns, looks at* CHARLIE *and* MANDY.

CHARLIE. She's looking at us.

The BILLYS *exit, followed by* ANN. CHARLIE *tries to find a position onstage where he can continue to watch* ANN *offstage.* MANDY *goes up to* CHARLIE, *touches him gently on the arm.*

MANDY. Don't let the devil steal your eyes away.

CHARLIE *doesn't look at her, his gaze fixed offstage on* ANN.

CHARLIE. She's stopped.

MANDY. Haven't you got something better to look at?

CHARLIE. She's turned round.

MANDY. You think you're looking but you're not, you're drowning.

CHARLIE. It's Ann.

MAX. I don't comprehend this. To me this passes – . This is past – .

CHARLIE. She's coming back.

MAX. I've passed out.

CHARLIE *takes up a position to await* ANN's *arrival.* ANN *enters, talking over her shoulder.*

ANN. I seem to be the only one that can see ahead to what's coming. Ambulances? They have to wait till a thing's happened don't they. Till after everything's all over and they might as well not have effn bothered. – Oh look who it is. My daughter Mandy. Has she been showing you her character, Charlie?

CHARLIE. She's been trying to save me, haven't you, Mandy?

ANN. What have you been saving him for, later?

CHARLIE. She's very kindly offered to take me back to your house, Ann.

ANN. Has she? You watch your step, Charlie, she's trickier than a mirror – see when it looks at ye? Oh look. Here come my two workers, Charlie.

The BILLYS *come on carrying the wardrobe.*

ANN. Are you two going to follow me all the way home !

BILLY 1. What way are you going, Ann!

ANN. No, Billy!

BILLY 1. 'No'?

ANN. I'm no walking the two miles home behind a stupid big thing like that .

BILLY 1. Could you no have thought of that before?

ANN. Fate, Charlie.

CHARLIE. We meet again, eh?

ANN. You can *explain* it.

CHARLIE; You can *explain* it.

ANN. Still doesn't *explain* it.

CHARLIE. Fate.

BILLY 1. Can we put this down, Billy?

BILLY 2. I'm waiting on Ann to tell me, Billy.

CHARLIE. Would you no be better transporting it by van?

BILLY 1. Yeah. You got one?

CHARLIE. We must know somebody between us that's got a van some kinna transport.

They don't.

BILLY 2. I've got a brother-in-law in Germany drives a big artic.

BILLY 1. Billy, can we put this down?

BILLY 2. Billy, we put it down: then what?

BILLY 1. Then I demolish ye, ya big wall.

CHARLIE. I mean, if there's any way, Ann, I can help you . . . not *help* . . . if there's any way I can not *help* you *something* you, then I'd be only too glad.

ANN. Uch, Fate, Charlie: you can't escape it. I had these two sons. First Robert hung himself. Then Martin?

ANN *imagines she's got the sequence in the wrong order and 'corrects' herself.*

ANN. What did I say there? First *Robert* hung himself. Then *Martin*. I don't know what was the bigger shock. It was a shock the first time wasn't it. Then when we found *Martin* in the boys' wardrobe like his twin brother that was another shock. Like seeing things. You can't blame Robert. He wasn't to know the future was he. You can't blame Martin either, he was only copying his twin. You're white as a sheet, Charlie, what did I say, did I say something wrong?

CHARLIE. No. It's just . . . some days you know you're being told something. Y'know? You're being told to get real or something. Y'know? How though?

BILLY 1. Talk to Billy. He's so real it's untrue.

BILLY 2. I might no be clever, Billy, but I can lift heavy things,

ANN. You just follow your instincts, Charlie. Well! I'll go and look for something else I forgot. Mandy, will you go home and open the door for them? – I'll see you two later. – I hope I bump into you again, Charlie. – I'm going to throw myself into the arms of Fate.

ANN *crosses the stage back in the direction of the Barras.*

BILLY 1. Ann, will you – . Billy, will you – .

CHARLIE. Is she OK? Should someone no go after her?

ANN *has now exited.*

CHARLIE. Should some bastard not, I think someone should go after her, Mandy.

MANDY. Why?

CHARLIE. I'll go after her then, if no other bastard's going to.

MAX. Charlie son, have you lost your sense of smell? Have you lost your sense of foreboding? Because I swear, Charlie, you go and loss yourself in ghostland you will be beset, beset, Charlie, and torn to pieces by your own hands.

CHARLIE *exits after* ANN. BILLY 1 *drops his end of the wardrobe.* MAX *loses the place.*

MAX. OK, Christian? I've been as Christian as I can be without actually striking you. OK? You stand there while I look for a weapon, and it'll be a big blind one-eyed lump of wood with a fucking five-inch nail where its cyclops eye should be and we'll see who's blind then!

MAX *hunts around for a weapon.*

BILLY 1. OK, Billy: lift.

The two BILLYS *lift the big wardrobe and set off in the same direction as* ANN. MAX *locates a suitable weapon and advances on* MANDY.

MAX. OK, Christian? I promised you . . .

MANDY. Not the now, Max . . .

MAX. . . . this is the bastard cyclops is going to explain violence to you . . . !

MANDY. . . . we're going to the bookie's . . .

MAX. . . . violence that I can't seem to explain to you, except by returning to the original Greek!

MAX *drops his weapon.* MANDY *sets off in the direction of the bookie's.*

MANDY. We can get something to eat on the way.

MAX. You're okay you. You're alright by the way. Charlie, man: the smell of bad luck off the holy jinx creeps like a sweating urinal, I have to sleep the same room as him because he's frightened he gets the fears! You're okay you. You've doubled your money, put it that way.

MANDY's *gone.*

MAX. You've got ten notes on yir tail. Charlie, man: I've been carrying that thing all day.

MAX *exits after* MANDY.

Scene Seven

Another corner of The Barras. A couple of handcarts with junk on them which may just be temporarily untended but look as if they've been abandoned for good. Only one of the stalls looks slightly more alive. It's decorated with heart-shaped crimson and silver balloons.

NANETTE *and* PROPHET JOHN *come on carting boxes of singles.* NANETTE's *a trader.* NANETTE's *got one box,* JOHN's *got four.*

NANETTE. The thing is John how literal I take things. Everything to me is as straightforward literal as the manna in the desert or the burning bush. So when you say once there was a woman I take that to mean once there was a woman, John. Am I right?

PROPHET JOHN. Yes.

NANETTE. I'm no jealous: (the Lord has been with me ever since I was a wee girl, he won't desert me now). So there was a woman.

PROPHET JOHN. Yes!

NANETTE. I'm just asking! – Cheesey peeps. – I'm only inquiring, John! – So what was she like?

PROPHET JOHN. She's dead.

NANETTE. Well I can't compete with that can I. I'm only here in the flesh. I'm only clothed like the lilies of the fields, finer than the robes of Solomon. – How did she die? – Eh?

PROPHET JOHN. 'Eh?'

NANETTE. Oh forget it then, effn forget it. If you cannae see what's in front of your eyes . . .

ANN *enters, looking behind her.*

ANN. Hi there, I'm looking for a single I lost.

NANETTE. Whatever it is we've got it here. This is all the singles here you've ever tried to forget, I cry just looking at the titles. Tell me a rotten single and I've got it.

ANN. Have you got Tom Jones doing The Skye Boat Song?

NANETTE. I could look for you. John, you away and speak to her by the upstairs café.

PROPHET JOHN *and* ANN *stare at each other.*

ANN. You're . . . He's . . .

NANETTE. Uh huh. On you go John hurry up!

PROPHET JOHN *exits.*

NANETTE. Did he 'speak' to you, dear? He 'speaks' to a few of us . . . eight or nine just. We call him Prophet John. Uh huh yes uh huh. When the spirit takes him he has wings like to Noah's dove, but when the spirit deserts him again he's like a slave.

NANETTE *is thumbing through a long box of old singles looking for the Tom Jones. Basically though she doubts its existence.*

NANETTE. The Skye Boat Song?

ANN. It's no for me.

NANETTE. Are you sure?

ANN. Yes!

NANETTE. The one about Bonny Prince Charlie they made us sing at school to teach us how Scottish we were?

ANN. He loaned it to me . . . my boyfriend . . .

NANETTE. Aw.

ANN. . . . I *predicted* I'd ruin it. I left it lying out till it warped didn't I. Then I panicked, put it under the grill on just a low flame, to try and flatten it out again? That only seemed to make it worse.

NANETTE. I see.

She goes on looking. She sings the first verse of 'The Skye Boat Song' in a sort of questioning tone as much as to say, 'Are you sure you're thinking of the right song?'

Speed bonny boat, like a bird on the wing
'Onward!' the sailors cry.
Carry the lad that's born to be king
Over the sea to Skye . . . ?

Eff this. I can think of better things to do with my index finger! I'll see if it's listed. You look through that box there.

ANN *starts to look through a box of singles.*

ANN. Are they in any order?

NANETTE. It's just a whole load of rubbish dear people have flung out: what's the sense putting them in any order!

CHARLIE *enters.*

CHARLIE. Ann.

ANN. Charlie.

CHARLIE. I hope you don't mind me following you, Ann. I came just to say –

ANN. What?

CHARLIE. Ach. Nothing.

ANN. It's OK. Say it.

CHARLIE. It's just that I left the wife. So I've no right to even anything, mouth that I am. What I came to say is: sadness. Y'know? You marry, have a kid, leave them.

ANN. It's the order things happen in isn't it.

CHARLIE. What is?

ANN. Sadness. It's a jumble.

NANETTE. I don't see it listed. I don't mind trying to help you dear (we all need help don't we?) . . .

CHARLIE. I get confused as well, Ann (if that's any consolation to you, Ann) (can I call you Ann, Ann) . Why when there's so much sadness and confusion in the world can we not reach out and comfort each other.

ANN. It's not just the world is it. Even thc galaxies are drifting apart . . .

CHARLIE. . . . I know . . .

ANN. . . . What. chance have people got?

CHARLIE. I'm trying to get across to the Vicky. Yeah. My mammy's dying . . .

ANN. Aw.

CHARLIE. Yeah. She's no even my mammy. I thought she was my mammy till I came home from school one day and saw this nice lady sitting on the couch and my mammy said this is your mammy, Charlie, say hello. So I said hello, then I went out and played at . . . (kicking a ball against a wall) . . . till the long slow night came in. – It turned out my mammy was really my granny. Which explains why she's a hunner odds (seventy something).

ANN. Awwwwww. Chicory Tip.

CHARLIE. Aw yeah.

ANN. We used to think these singles were forever.

CHARLIE. What does forever mean anyway, am I right. I used to say that to Margaret Mary (the wife, left her), what does forever mean, Margaret Mary? That was half the problem with me and her, what she meant by forever and what I meant was two entirely different things. Ahch, what's it matter, it's over . . . Infinity . . . y'know? . . . infinity was beyond her. All I'm saying is (you're lovely by the way) all I'm saying is . . . it doesn't have to be forever.

ANN. Don't look now, here come my two deadly rivals.

The BILLYS *enter with the wardrobe, sweat pouring off them and out of breath.*

BILLY 1. OK, Billy? Can we put this thing down now?

BILLY 2 (*fucked*). Is it OK to put this thing down now, Ann?

ANN. If you want, Billy.

The BILLYS *put the wardrobe down.*

BILLY 1. OK, Ann? OK? All I need is a minute so can everyone no move for thirty seconds. OK, Ann? Because can I explain something, Ann: what the fuck *is* it with you today? I'm thirty three four now, most men have been married twice the time they're my age never mind none, so this is my big day too, right? We said that, didn't we. We said this was my big day too.

ANN. I know we did, Billy.

BILLY 1. Well can you stop treating me as though I'm Billy.

You even tell him you love him Ann, you even Ann sleep with him – so he thinks that means something doesn't he,

ANN. It does mean something .

BILLY 1. I *know* that. But how's he supposed to know you don't mean it the same way as you mean it with me when you treat me the exact same way as you treat him I mean, *I'm* perplexed, so how d'you think Billy feels?

BILLY 2. I feel fine, Ann.

CHARLIE. Are these two annoying you, Ann?

BILLY 1. I'm *perplexed,* Ann. Y'know? I'm fucking fucked actually.

ANN. Billy, if I could say what I wanted to say, if I could speak the words and hear myself saying them without the dogs of hell tearing my throat out, then I promise, I would. – I'm hoping Fate speaks. I've cast my bread upon the waters and I have to wait and see what the waters bring back up.

PROPHET JOHN *enters and gives a single to* ANN.

PROPHET JOHN. Here. I fun it by the upstairs café.

ANN. Oh god.

BILLY 1. What is it, Ann?

ANN *takes the single and crosses over to* BILLY 2.

ANN. Billy, look what I found. I don't know if it's Fate or what it is, I do believe Fate speaks . . . I could wish she didn't and maybe we don't always understand her . . . which is maybe just as well at times . . . but when Fate speaks . . .

She gives him the single.

ANN. . . . . what we say or don't say, when Fate speaks our poor words fall short.

BILLY 2. I don't believe it.

NANETTE. Och . . . it's not unusual.

BILLY 2. Naw. That was the second single the so-called white man with the Motown voice released. This is something else. This is an all-time one-off recording also from 1965 that doesnae even exist.

NANETTE. I thought that.

BILLY 2. Decca denied this single down the phone, so did Tom's manager. I got a wee bit obsessed about it, y'know? Latterly the T. J. Newsletter refused to correspond with me on the subject and my wife deserted me for another fan. I had a single that nobody could explain how it had come to be, or why. Then I got a letter from an Italian called Umberto Eco. It turns out The Skye Boat Song was only ever released by an independent label in Naples that got liquidated shortly after, and I had one of the few copies still extant. That's why I was upset when Ann toasted it. I went back to her after a fortnight. I couldn't even fall out with her in the end. That was a shock to me. I couldn't even fall out with her. I went back and told her, she was the all-time one-off of all time.

BILLY 1. He can't see it Ann.

BILLY 2. She was the all-time one-off of all time.

BILLY 1. It's code, Billy: think. Why's she being so nice to you for christssake.

BILLY 2. We have our own code, Billy . . . . . . nothing's broken it yet . . .

NANETTE. How much would you say that single was worth, Billy?

MANDY *enters, followed by* MAX.

MANDY. Charlie. I'm still shaking. I won so much money I don't know if it's good.

MAX. The first off at Newmarket, Charlie son.

MANDY. We placed the first and second. I won so much money I don't know if it's good.

NANETTE. Hallelujah.

BILLY 2. Ahch! We're all winners today!

ANN. How much did you win?

MAX. A monkey-load, an effn ape-load.

CHARLIE. How much?

MAX. Bollocks plenty, put it that way.

CHARLIE. I suppose, on the question of how to split it Mandy, I suppose half . . .

MANDY. . . . . half . . .

CHARLIE. . . . . stake-money was yours and half, the other half . . .

MANDY. . . . . was the fiver you lost when you gave me that stupit bet, I suppose. I suppose if I thought the money was a sign to you to believe in me . . . and lead you down the path . . .

ANN. I warned you, Charlie. Tricky? She's trickier than a crowd of sheep (see when they run at ye).

MANDY. Do you want to count it?

MANDY *crosses to* CHARLIE *and hands him the wad of cash, which he proceeds to count.*

MANDY. We could go and get you some new togs.

CHARLIE. Yeah.

ANN. How much is it, Charlie?

NANETTE. How much is it, Charlie?

CHARLIE. (Fucking) back off (fuckssake).

MANDY. Back off, he can't breathe.

CHARLIE. This is . . . what's the word, Mandy . . . I'm moved.
    Y'know? I cannae even count right.

    MARGARET MARY *enters*.

MARGARET MARY. Charlie.

CHARLIE. Margaret Mary.

MARGARET MARY. Can I speak to you a minute?

CHARLIE. Here I am. I'm listening.

    MARGARET MARY *would like to speak to* CHARLIE *in
    private.* CHARLIE'*s not interested. He's holding onto the (as
    yet undivided) cash.*

MARGARET MARY. I'm sorry about your mammy. I'm sorry
    I didnae believe you this morning. After you came to see me
    I went inside and phoned your sister and it turned out your
    mammie was taken bad. So I followed you here.

CHARLIE. What can I say? I tell you my mammy's dying and you
    don't believe me? I was in tears. You were in tears.

MARGARET MARY. I know.

CHARLIE. What did you think we were crying for?

MARGARET MARY. It was sad .

CHARLIE. Sad?! (All I want to do is break my heart. You'd think
    that would be easy. Apparently naw, apparently it's a long
    bastard slog.) Sad?!

MARGARET MARY. I've been crying ever since to make up for
    it. I feel so sorry for ye, Charlie. It's times like this you need yir
    family isn't it and to know they're thinking about you and
    hoping you'll come through and that if you want anything
    Charlie or need anything you only have to ask Charlie, because
    I'm still your wife, no matter.

CHARLIE. Sad?! (I've lost the place here.) Sad?! Because I don't
    want to humiliate you, Margaret Mary, in front of complete
    strangers, but you're humiliating yourself, sweetheart. I'm
    bewildered. I am. When the former person you made your
    vows to treats you like – then let the shad come up and cover
    me and take me down – because I'm bereaved of excuses for

her. I come to you to let you know my own mammie is dying and you think I'm lying in order to get a tenner off ye.

MARGARET MARY *turns her back on him, embarrassed, humiliated, wanting this to stop.*

I'm sorry Margaret Mary but it's true. I wish it wasnae true as well Margaret Mary, I really do. You gave me a tenner, Margaret Mary! You know what I'm saying? You gave me a tenner!! What does that make me? I'm no even going to try and imagine what it makes me. Because when the former person you made your vows to turns her back on you then let the sun peck my eyes out as far as I'm concerned because darkness has covered the earth and money? Money? I'll money ye! I'll give you money!

CHARLIE *tears the wad of money in half.*

MANDY. Charlie!

CHARLIE *tears the money in four.*

MANDY. Charlie!

CHARLIE *tears the money in eight, and throws it in the air to fall like confetti.*

ANN. Oh god!

NANETTE. Cheesey peeps!

MAX. Oh Charlie.

BILLY 2. I hope he's going to clear that mess up.

ANN. What happened, Mandy?

MANDY. You saw him.

ANN. Did he tear it up?

NANETTE. I think so.

ANN. It was like violence or something, wasn't it. The way it stands out, bright as confetti after the rain . . .

CHARLIE *crosses to the wardrobe, upon which* BILLY 1 *is sitting disconsolate.*

CHARLIE. OK Billy, we've got a job to do: let's get this thing shifted – come on come on come on son – shape up and show some effn dignity.

BILLY 1. I'll see you back at the house, Ann. This is to show you that I understand. You've said things to Billy in the past that maybe you shouldn't've said but you've said them therefore: whatever: etcetera that I don't need to say. Don't take too long though because I'm beginning to start no being able to focus or even see things. OK?

BILLY 1 *walks away home.*

CHARLIE. What's up wi you? Eh, what's up wi him? OK Billy, it's down to us two. Come on, Billy, come on, wake up son or you'll get left behind.

BILLY 2 *crosses to help* CHARLIE *shift the wardrobe.*

BILLY 2. I'll see you back at the house, Ann,

CHARLIE. Come on, Billy; before the wind blows through me.

BILLY 2 *and* CHARLIE *exit with the wardrobe.* MAX *starts picking up the torn pieces of money.*

ANN. How much are your knickers, pet?

NANETTE. 50p a pair, fresh from M and S this morning. They don't come cheaper 'less you knock them yourself.

ANN. Give us ten. So how much is that I owe ye . . . ?

NANETTE. . . . Nanette. Ten pair of knickers is a fiver and a fiver for the Tom Jones,

ANN. Right, we better get on . . . What is it your name is, pet?

MARGARET MARY. Margaret Mary. You're the woman lives next close along from me.

ANN (*shocked*). Oh, so I am! Well, we better get on . . .

MARGARET MARY. I'm sorry about your two boys. The two boys that went and hung themselves?

ANN. Oh uh huh. So are you Charlie's wife?

MARGARET MARY. I believe marriage is for life. Do you?

ANN. Yes. Oh uh huh. That's why I'm no sure if I'm in favour of it.

MARGARET MARY. I believe marriage is for life. Charlie said to me this one time he wanted a divorce. I went Charlie, even if you're no married to me I'd still be married to you!

ANN. Anyway. We better get on, Margaret Mary: I'm maybe getting married this afternoon.

NANETTE. D'you hear that, John – a wedding!

ANN. We'll see we'll see we'll see: I've asked the minister to come round and if it happens it happens. I'm under no illusions. Anyway you're all very welcome, Nanette, the more the merrier, Margaret Mary, 36/3 Arcadia Street, Nanette: no promises but whatever happens something will happen: there'll probably be a . . . (an every-man-for-himself-type-thing) . . .

NANETTE. D'you hear that, John – a buffet!

ANN. Och, it's a chance to wear a hat, isn't it. So will we see you there?

MAX. What about me?

ANN. What about you?

MAX. See Charlie (I feel sad for the deaf blind jinx creep, he's a pal). Look, if ye want me to come along, y'know? Because fair enough, I will then: I've carried him this long . . .

ANN, MANDY, *and* MARGARET MARY *exit*. MAX *traipses after them*.

PROPHET JOHN *and* NANETTE *start to pack up, close their stall*.

NANETTE. I still don't believe that single. I can't imagine it or hear it or picture what it sounds like. I don't know where the hell you got it from. – So d'you fancy a wedding? I think we should go. We've been invited. She must be a bit desperate or she wouldn't have asked us. So, d'you fancy a wedding. Eh?

PROPHET JOHN. 'Eh?'

NANETTE. Eh, miserable?

PROPHET JOHN. I do.

ACT TWO

There are two locations; the backgreen and the boys' bedroom.

Mainly the backgreen should create a sense of spaciousness and light. The wardobe from Act One has been left out here, abandoned to the sun.

The boys' bedroom is very small and is wholly dominated by a big wardrobe in which two boys have hung themselves.

The boys' bedroom is above and beyond the backgreen.

It's later the same day, about three o clock on a hot afternoon. There is the sound off of a party. Then someone puts on a record and we hear the pulsing intro of a song which turns into Tom Jones' legendary version of The Skye Boat Song.

BILLY 1 enters the backgreen from stage left, dressed as a bridegroom. He's carrying BILLY 2's suitcases which he puts on the ground then sits on, to wait. After a bit MARGARET MARY comes out. In the conversation that follows they don't really engage with each other, their minds engaged with what's happening elsewhere.

MARGARET MARY. So.

BILLY 1. Good enough.

MARGARET MARY. D'you think so?

BILLY 1. I'm just sitting here waiting on Billy to come and retrieve his suitcases.

   Beat.

MARGARET MARY. What time's the minister coming?

BILLY 1. He's late. – So. Good enough. So how's it going up there? Everybody enjoying theirselves?

MARGARET MARY. Uch . . .

BILLY 1. Naw naw, good enough. It's a wedding! It's a happy event! And (good enough) you want people to share your happiness don't ye.

MARGARET MARY. I don't mind people being happy. It's a happy event. I just think you should've the ceremony first then go wild. What's the minister going to say when he gets here and sees all the carry-on.

BILLY 1. Ahch, they're only carrying on.

Beat.

MARGARET MARY. It's Charlie I feel for. You know Ann and Mandy are only having a carry-on with him and I know Ann and Mandy are only having a carry-on with him but by the time Charlie realises Ann and Mandy are only having a carry-on with him he'll be a wee pile of bones that they've left.

BILLY 1. Ahch well. Good enough.

Beat.

MARGARET MARY. It's Charlie I feel for. He's in fairyland as it is without (dope) and (carry-on). It's time he woke up, got a suit and remembered who he is. – He's a different man in his suit. You should've seen him at his wedding. He looked so handsome. I looked nice as well but he looked so handsome. When he made his vows he was that serious he looked like a young priest. – It's Charlie I feel for. He's like the man in the gospels that found a treasure in a field. He's delighted, so he leaves the treasure where he found it and goes off and gets drunk. Then next day he goes looking for the field again and can't find it.

Beat.

BILLY 1. I wonder very much Marie-Therese if you would leave me alone here.

MARGARET MARY. I'm Margaret Mary.

BILLY 1. I wonder very much Mary Margaret if you would leave me alone here.

ANN *enters the boys' bedroom in a bad mood, slamming the door behind her.*

ANN. She's been dogging my steps all bloody day – the wee minx!

MARGARET MARY *doesn't move.*

MARGARET MARY. Where's the ceremony to be?

BILLY 1. Out here.

MARGARET MARY. Out here?

BILLY 1. Ann always wanted to be married in a garden.

MARGARET MARY. Aw.

BILLY 1. Yeah (y'know). nice.

MARGARET MARY *still doesn't want to go.*

MARGARET MARY. I'll wish you all the best then.

MARGARET MARY *exits in the direction of the house.*

BILLY 1 *crosses to the wardrobe. A strong light comes onto the wardrobe in the boys' bedroom where* ANN *is now sitting on the bed.* BILLY 1 *leans his head against the wardrobe.*

BILLY 1. Ann? Ann? Are you thinking about me? – Remember the time you phoned me from your house. 'Billy? It's me. I can't speak: I've got Billy here.' Then you put the phone down. Dead, nothing. – That's the difference between me and Billy: all the different things I heard in your voice, all the different things you couldn't say. – I wish you'd get ready, Ann. Put on some wee thing you've never worn for Billy, one tiny wee thing Ann you've never worn for Billy and never will. And I promise: when today's all over you'll look back and see, you were only ever faithful to me.

In the boys' bedroom, ANN *starts talking to someone outside the door.*

ANN. I don't know what to say to you. Ugly? I didn't know what ugly was till you. Don't pretend you're no there. I can hear you. I can hear you not breathing. – Creep, creep, creep. – Don't pretend you're not there, Mandy, I heard you creeping up (you've been on the creep all day). – It's Charlie I feel for. It's Charlie my heart goes out to. What chance has he got with you sitting on his knee pointing your tits at him. I hope you don't think I'm competing with ye. I'm just trying to make sure Charlie has a pleasant time. I stumbled and fell onto his knees by accident – and don't give me one of your looks! There can only be one of everything, Mandy. There can only be one of each thing. Don't let the twins confuse you. The twins were the same thing. It was the same thing with the twins. Don't jumble everything up till it's all the same hideous mess.

MANDY. Have you made your decision yet?

ANN. Eh?

MANDY. Have you made your decision yet?

ANN. Yes I've made my decision. Are you happy?

MANDY. What decision did you make?

ANN. Wait and see. So you're happy then?

MANDY. I'm happy if you're happy.

ANN. Is that what you say to your men? 'I'm happy if you're happy.'

MANDY. Are you happy?

Beat.

ANN. Nine years. Nine bloody years. I don't blame Martin. I can't blame Martin. He was only copying his twin. He wanted to be with his twin didn't he. He wanted to be the same thing as his twin. Faithfulness. That's what Martin teaches us. Faithfulness. – We can all learn lessons from the dead, Mandy. – Do you hear me, Mandy?

MANDY. I'm going back to the living-room.

ANN. Mandy! I'm warning you!

ANN *gets up off the bed, crosses to the door, opens it.*
MANDY's *gone.*

BILLY 1. I'm ready when you're ready, Ann.

ANN *exits after* MANDY.

PROPHET JOHN *and* NANETTE *enter the back-green from
the direction of the shops.*

NANETTE. We're here, we're here, I hope we've no missed any
of the excitement. Oh here, I'm quite excited, would ye believe
that? I'm in as big a tizz as the bride. D'you like my hat? You
don't think it's too orange? I mean, it's no that I want to show
my colours but I didnae want to buy a hat I'd only wear the
once, where this is a hat I'll get good use out of. – So! Where's
the bride and groom?

BILLY 1. I'm the groom. Billy.

NANETTE. Oh look, John, this is the groom!

PROPHET JOHN. Can I shake your hand, Billy? Billy, can I shake
your hand? Billy, can I shake your hand? Billy, can I shake
your hand? Billy, can I shake your hand?

NANETTE. He wants to shake your hand, Billy.

PROPHET JOHN *and* BILLY *shake hands.* JOHN *is looking
at* BILLY *like he wants to eat him.*

PROPHET JOHN. You're very welcome, Billy. I have prepared a
sacrifice, I have consecrated my guests. Welcome.

NANETTE. Why don't we go inside and have some food, John?
Eh?

PROPHET JOHN. 'Eh?'

PROPHET JOHN *doesn't want to go inside having found his
prey in* BILLY 1 *whom he shadows throughout the rest of this
scene.*

BILLY 2 *enters the back-green from stage left the direction of
the house. He goes to pick up his suitcases.*

BILLY 2. I've come to get my suitcases, Billy.

BILLY 1. Confident, Billy?

BILLY 2. You only have to observe the facts. You?

BILLY 1. Why don't you leave your suitcases till we talk, Billy?

BILLY 2. Will you stop calling me Billy, Billy . . .

BILLY 1. Can we talk?

BILLY 2. . . . let's leave our personalities out of this!

BILLY 1. That suits me.

BILLY 2 *puts down his suitcases.*

BILLY 1. I can say what I've got to say in seven sentences. OK? Then it's up to you. OK?

BILLY 2. I'm OK, you OK?

BILLY 1. Can we be pleasant then?

BILLY 2. Talk.

BILLY 1. Fine. – I don't dislike you, Billy . . .

BILLY 2 *goes mental, comes forward towards the other* BILLY, *hand in inside pocket of his jacket (i.e. as if he's loaded, got a chib or whatever).*

BILLY 2. I'll chisel your eyes out!

BILLY 1. . . . what the fuck . . .

BILLY 2. I'll hammer this up your nose, pal.

BILLY 1. . . . fuck did I say!

BILLY 2. 'I don't dislike you, Billy.' I'll jump on your face, son.

BILLY 1. I was trying to be pleasant (ya arse) I apologise. Can I take it back? OK? I take it back. Can we start again?

BILLY 2. Don't call me Billy.

BILLY 1. I've apologised!

BILLY 2. Keech-features.

BILLY 1. Right. Fine. I'll start again. OK? I don't dislike you. OK? Why should I. Many many ways we're very similar.

BILLY 2. Haw.

BILLY 1. Many many ways (what did you say?) many many ways we're (haw?) many many ways we're (tragic). Identical.

BILLY 2. I hope you know what you're talking about, Billy.

BILLY 1. Ann. OK?

BILLY 2. Keep it to the facts, OK?

BILLY 1. OK OK, Ann, OK? So. I'm confident. You say you're confident.

BILLY 2. I'm confident.

BILLY 1. OK then: Ann doesn't marry me today, I walk from here to death's door and I don't come back ever, because I won't know the way any more. You're confident, you back out till after today when she's all yours. You've got your suitcases: are you going to walk? – Are you going to walk?

MAX *enters pursued by a bear. The bear is* CHARLIE. CHARLIE *is followed by* ANN *and* MANDY, *then* MARGARET MARY, *all from the direction of the house.*

CHARLIE. Max!

ANN. Charlie!

CHARLIE. Max!

MANDY. Charlie!

CHARLIE. Tell me what you said, ya toxin! (He opens his mouth I try to not inhale.) Tell me what you said, ya pollutant!

BILLY 2 *picks up his suitcases and starts to walk but in the direction of the house rather than the shops.*

BILLY 1. That's the wrong direction, my friend.

MAX. You heard what I said.

BILLY 1. So therefore you don't love her then.

CHARLIE. You're dead.

MAX. I said when are you going to wake up?

BILLY 2. You're dead.

MAX. Am I.

BILLY 1 *backs off the* BILLY *stand-off to look for a weapon.*

MARGARET MARY. Will I jump next door and find you a suit, Charlie?

CHARLIE. Margaret Mary! It won't fit!

MARGARET MARY. It will!

CHARLIE. It won't!

MARGARET MARY *exits stage left.* BILLY 1 *has now found a weapon, big lump of metal, with which he faces* BILLY 2.

CHARLIE. What's going on here! Can I call for a period of calm? First Max, now her?!

ANN. We'll find you a suit easy enough, if that's what you want. Billy's got two suits.

BILLY 1. OK, Billy?

BILLY 2 *stands there for a moment then backs off to look for a weapon.* ANN *crosses to* BILLY 2's *suitcases and starts to look through them for a suit.*

BILLY 2 *has picked up a bottle which he's considering using as a weapon.*

BILLY 1. OK, Billy?

BILLY 2. I won't keep you long, Billy.

BILLY 1. Don't keep me long, Billy.

BILLY 2. I won't keep you long, Billy.

BILLY 1. He's thinking.

BILLY 2. Is he?

BILLY 2 *breaks the bottle and comes forward to face* BILLY 1. *Meanwhile* ANN *has found a suit which might be suitable.*

ANN. Billy!

BILLY 1 (*playing 'cool'*). So what are you saying, Billy?

ANN. Billy!

BILLY 1 (*'cool'*). So you're not going to walk then?

ANN. Billy! Has this suit been to the laundrette lately? I think it has, Charlie.

Getting no reply, ANN *crosses to* CHARLIE *and holds the brown suit against him to see how it is for size.*

BILLY 2 (*playing 'reluctant'*). I'm going to have to cut you a fresh mouth, Billy.

BILLY 1 (*'cool'*). Face it, Billy: you're a nice person. Even Ann says it.

BILLY 2 (*'cool'*). He's upset. What you upset about, Billy?

BILLY 1 (*'cool'*). I'm fine, Billy.

BILLY 2 (*'cool'*). What you upset about, ugly?

BILLY 1 (*'cool'*). I'm a wee bit pushed for time today, Billy, can we commence?

BILLY 2 (*'cool'*). You do everything in a hurry, eh Billy? Even Ann says it.

CHARLIE *is holding the brown suit against his body while* ANN *has backed off to get a better look – into the path of the two* BILLYS.

ANN. . . . I don't know . . . . . . I can't seem to make up my mind . . .

BILLY 1. Out the way, Ann.

BILLY 2. Ann, out the way.

BILLY 1. Ann!

BILLY 2. Out the way, Ann!

ANN *notices the* BILLYS *are close to a fight.*

ANN. I'm trying to make up my mind, Billy!

CHARLIE. Calm down, Billy. OK Billy, calm it.

MANDY. Charlie, you come out the way!

CHARLIE. Calm down or I'll sort the two of you out.

BILLY 2. Out the way, I can't see him.

BILLY 1. Out the way you.

BILLY 2.: Where's the bull?

BILLY 1. Or I'll mistake you for Billy.

BILLY 2. He'll stampede all over you!

BILLY 1. I'll stamp you into the ground! I'll rip out your teeth and sow them into the earth! I'll obliterate you!

> STUART *the minister enters stage right from the direction of the shops, taking in the scene almost without a pause.*

STUART. OK, we ready? I'm running late (I've got a date tonight) spent the last four hours with a woman wanted to see me said she was depressed (the reason I'm late). I just shouted at her. I said you've got seven kids, you live in a toilet and your man gets out of jail next week, of course you're depressed! The trick at a wedding's to remember their names. How you doing, wee man (I call her wee man). I know the bride: how are you, Ann?

ANN. Uch . . .

STUART. Are you as nervous as me?

ANN. I suppose every bride's the same (that's getting married).

STUART. Last minute doubts?

ANN. Emm . . .

STUART. OK, Billy?

> STUART *goes to shake* BILLY 1's *hand.* BILLY 1 *drops his weapon.*

STUART. Good. You me and Ann are going inside for a blether. Shift!

> STUART *indicates with his thumb for* BILLY 1 *and* ANN *to move it, and off they go stage left.*

STUART. The rest of you stay here till we see what the story is. There's ten commandments, far too many, right? Pick one and try and keep it till I get back.

> STUART *exits.* PROPHET JOHN *and* NANETTE *follow.*

NANETTE. John, will you try and remember you're a guest.

> CHARLIE *focus is off-stage, with* ANN: *concerned about her fate.*

CHARLIE. I'm no too keen on the minister. I've got a good mind to go and stick one on him. Eh? Because he's a minister that entitles him to be ignorant? Ann can do without that (the peril she's in) she can do without being ordered around by an ignorant wee nyaff.

MANDY. Och, he's OK.

CHARLIE. He's not OK, Mandy. He's inexorable. – Has Ann used him before.

MANDY. Yeah. Twice.

BILLY 2 *leaves his suitcases and exits in the direction of the house.*

CHARLIE. If there's one thing that upsets me, it's ignorance.

MANDY. I'm hot, are you hot? D'you fancy an ice-lolly?

CHARLIE. You got any money?

MANDY. Yeah.

CHARLIE. It's a bit sticky getting.

MANDY. I'll treat you.

CHARLIE. OK, wee man. I maybe do need to cool down.

MANDY. C'mon then.

MAX. I'll wait here. I'll be here when you get back. OK? – The seasons I can contend with, Charlie. The seasons I can be philosophical about. I'd be happier if something blotted out the sun for good so that was that and we didn't have to live with false hopes but the best I can do meantime is (fuck the seasons) pay no heed to them.

CHARLIE. What's up with you?

MANDY. Does he want an ice-lolly too?

CHARLIE. What's up with you, torn face?

MAX *gets some of the torn-up money out of his pocket and flings it at* CHARLIE.

MAX. That's what's up with me! When are you going to wake up and come out of the land of strangers, Charlie? When are you going to wake up and acknowledge your debts? I came up big today, I placed a first and second at accumulated odds of 33/2 and won a monkey-load of money which I handed over to you, Charlie, to divide, Charlie, divide according as you saw fit and now I can't put it together again!

Beat.

CHARLIE. I owe ye money, is that it?

MAX. I estimate twenty notes. That's how I see it.

CHARLIE. Yeah?

MAX. That's my interpretation.

CHARLIE. When do you want it?

MAX. When can you get it?

CHARLIE. When do you want it?

MAX. I don't want to be unreasonable.

CHARLIE. Would a few days hence be acceptable?

MAX. You got any securities you can give me meantime?

CHARLIE. Meantime?

MAX. I'm the loser meantime. I've got the worry.

CHARLIE. Correct. – C'mon, wee man.

MANDY and CHARLIE exit in the direction of the shops.

MAX. I'm the one that has to calculate for the both of us!

CHARLIE's gone.

MAX. I don't know how you're going to account for yourself today.

MAX crosses the stage, shouts up at MARGARET MARY's house.

MAX. Margaret Mary? Margaret Mary?

MAX exits in the direction of the house.

There's a knock on the door in the boys bedroom. Then another knock. Then in comes PROPHET JOHN followed by NANETTE.

NANETTE. John. I don't think we should be here. – This is a bedroom, John.

She closes the door behind her, maybe goes to sit on the bed.

NANETTE. I don't see a wedding do you. She's got plenty suitors, I'll say that much (she's got more men than sense). She's got more men than places to put them all. – I think we should go, John. I don't know what I see but I don't see a wedding. And I don't much like what I do see. D'you hear me, John? Eh? We're here as guests today.

PROPHET JOHN goes up to the wardrobe and knocks on it.

PROPHET JOHN. Speak, prophet!

NANETTE. What is it, John? Is it the spirit? Is he close? Is he strong?

PROPHET JOHN. Speak, prophet!

The wardrobe rebuffs him.

PROPHET JOHN. He says 'No!' He says 'Go!' He says 'Eff off!'
They have run into the arms of the goddess. They have
committed abominations. They have worshipped Asherah and
performed rites.

Danced like wine!
Red like wine!
Like skin turned outside in!
Like the little knot, the little knot that won't untie.
They danced like wine!
Red like wine!
They saw visions!
Bees!
- clambered out of the sticky sun.
Bees!
- clambered out of the sticky sun.
He stands in front of the wardrobe and opens his arms to it.
Open your arms, sun!
Open your arms, sun!
Open your arms, sun!

The PROPHET *falls onto his knees, then lies on the floor and
tries to curl up.* NANETTE *covers him with something, then
goes and sits on the bed.*

NANETTE. It's OK, John. It's OK, son. You'll be OK. You'll be
OK in a minute. Do you want me to talk to you? You keep
quiet for a minute. Will I tell you a dream I had? It was a valley
and it was up to its waist in bones. I was lying there on top of
the bones and I was nothing but a skeleton myself. When all of
a sudden there's an avalanche. An avalanche of bones falls on
the valley like a deluge and I get pushed under. And when I
come to the surface again the valley is up to its neck in bones.
It's nice and peaceful. My bones are all broken and I can see
them, scattered here and there, shining in the sun. – You can
rest there for a bit. Then we'll skeedaddle. OK?

MANDY *and* CHARLIE *enter stage right from the shops,
with ice-lollies. They wander on in silence . . . together but not
really . . .* CHARLIE's *focus is in the direction of the house,
where* ANN *is.*

CHARLIE. I hope Ann's OK. – Silence. – I hope she's (I hope I'm
wrong) I hope this silence isn't ominous. – I'm trying to think
my way into her mind. Y'know? Her past.

MANDY. Y' can only inquire so much.

CHARLIE. The mind . . . ?

MANDY. Mmm.

CHARLIE. The mind only goes so far . . .

MANDY. A healthy mind.

CHARLIE. The mind only (I'm out of my depth here) the mind only goes so far till it's out of its depth? Yeah. I see that.

MANDY. A healthy mind varies its obsessions.

Beat.

CHARLIE. I'm a thinker to my cost. First Robert then Martin. What did I say there? First Robert, then Martin. And nobody found a reason?

MANDY. Uh huh.

CHARLIE. Uh huh?

MANDY. Mmm.

CHARLIE. Uh huh naw or uh huh aye?

MANDY. It all came out at the fatal inquiry.

CHARLIE. They said a reason?

MANDY. Yeah.

CHARLIE. Yeah?

MANDY. Yeah.

CHARLIE. What?

MANDY. They said Robert was unhappy.

CHARLIE. Right. And was he?

MANDY. Yeah. Then it turned out we knew he was unhappy and we'd never done nothing about it. Then when Martin went and done it as well that was easy, he even left a note. He said he hoped he'd see us both soon.

She's won his attention now. Physically they are quite close.

CHARLIE. You're some soldier, wee man.

MANDY. I don't normally get personal like this.

CHARLIE. I shouldnae even be here. I'll say that much for me.

MANDY. You should.

CHARLIE. I know. I know that. It's like 'What am I doing here?' You know? Whether whether I'm deregulated or something – I don't exclude that Mandy I can't exclude that I don't exclude anything which is maybe why I'm so deregulated . . . So, whether whether I'm deregulated or not . . .

MANDY. So you feel . . .

CHARLIE. Yeah. I do.

MANDY. You feel . . .

CHARLIE. I'm hypnotised.

MANDY. I'm glad. I thought you might be too weak. Jesus says
'Follow me!'

CHARLIE. She's beautiful. You're lovely too.

Beat.

MANDY. That's not what you said when we were sitting on my
bed.

CHARLIE. What did I say when we were sitting on your bed?

MANDY. I see.

CHARLIE. I remember Max came in and he said something.

MANDY. Forget it.

CHARLIE. I don't take it back, I'm just asking what I said.

MANDY. Aw don't greet! Is my character too strong? Jesus says
'Follow me!' What's her character? – she's got two men, that's
her character. She believes in numbers. I mean, she believes in
numbers (the more the merrier.) Or then she tries to improve
her character because it's so weak so she gets three men. – Fine
okay fine, 's fine. You're weak, I'm strong; you're lonely, I'll
be with you; you're lost and I'll save you.

Beat.

CHARLIE. I'm trying to think what to say. – See Robert and
Martin (which is admirable). See the (Robert and Martin)
questions I asked you.

MANDY. You asked me questions so I answered them.

CHARLIE. I admire that. What I'm saying, I went question and
you went answer (which, good enough).

MANDY. I was showing you my character.

CHARLIE. I admire that. What I'm saying, it's good you've
recovered.

Beat. Then MANDY *turns and exits.*

CHARLIE. What? Did I say something wrong? What did I say? I
said it's good you've recovered. I think that's what I said. Is
that no what I said? – I'm lost here. Does she want me to follow
her, is that it? Oh god. She's coming back.

MANDY *enters.*

MANDY. I tell you my secrets and you say them back to me in
different words?

CHARLIE. Naw, Mandy.

MANDY. I tell you my dreams and you interpret them?

CHARLIE. Naw, Mandy.

MANDY. I put my heart out on a dish and you lick it?

CHARLIE. Mandy –

MANDY. Where am I: Babylon? Here's another question: the king of Babylon had a dream so he summons all the wise men and fortune-tellers and says to them 'I had a dream. Tell me what it means.'

CHARLIE What was the dream?

MANDY. No! 'No!' the king says ('f you're so fucking smart!) 'Tell me what I dreamt first. Then you can interpret it.'

CHARLIE. . . . guess?

MANDY. Guess wrong and you're dead! 'You tell me what I dreamt then I'll know you're the One.' See? We don't worship the sun do we. The sun can no more think than we can. The sun can no more think ahead

CHARLIE. no more think ahead

MANDY. no more think

CHARLIE. think ahead than any other sunstroked bastard that can't think ahead

MANDY. the sun

CHARLIE. heatloss! (is all sun is)

MANDY. fat sun no more think ahead than think, all it wants to do is pish its fat shine away till it's over!

CHARLIE. You're crying.

MANDY. I'm not.

CHARLIE. She's crying.

MANDY. I am not crying.

CHARLIE. What are you crying for, snottery?

MANDY. . . . anybody can ask questions. I want someone that can see right through me, someone that can see the back of my face.

He's behind her. They are physically very close again. If she were to turn they would be as close as they could be without actually touching.

MANDY. So. Do you see now who I am?

CHARLIE. Yes. I do.

MANDY. And do you believe in me?

V

CHARLIE. Yes. I do.

MANDY. Say it then.

CHARLIE. I believe in you.

She embraces him.

In the boys' bedroom PROPHET JOHN *bestirs himself, gets up.*

NANETTE. OK? – Will we go? – I'm no jealous, John: I just think we should go and have a nice day somewhere. We'll see if we can sneak away when nobody's looking.

PROPHET JOHN *exits the boys' bedroom, followed by* NANETTE.

Out the back-green . . .

CHARLIE. Will we sit down?

MANDY. Where?

CHARLIE. Do you not want to?

MANDY. Uh huh. Do you want to?

CHARLIE. Out the way somewhere maybe?

ANN *enters the back-green.*

ANN. I see. Uch well.

CHARLIE. Ann.

ANN. Uh huh. Oh well. So long as you're happy.

CHARLIE. She's just been crying, Ann. Haven't you, wee barra.

ANN. So long as she's happy. How about you, Charlie?

CHARLIE. . . . . I'm happy if you're both happy . . .

ANN. Did you hear that, Mandy?

MANDY. Uh huh.

ANN. We're all in harmony.

CHARLIE. So, are we going to have a happy ending?

ANN *(fierce).* Are you fucking stupit?

CHARLIE. I meant, is there going to be a wedding?

ANN. Yes there's going to be a wedding! – Stuart says people think a wedding's a happy ending but it's not.

MARGARET MARY *enters, carrying a suit.* MAX *is with her.*

MARGARET MARY. Charlie. I brought you the suit.

CHARLIE. Margaret Mary: look: I appreciate the bother you're giving me. But just because a suit fits one man doesn't mean it's going to fit a completely different man, especially when one of the men is a twisted wee jobby like your da!

MARGARET MARY. Try it on.

CHARLIE. He's an animal, Mandy. The last thing I want to be seen dead in is his shitey brown suit.

MARGARET MARY. It's the suit you wore to your wedding isn't it.

Pause.

CHARLIE. It just shows how wrong ye can be.

MARGARET MARY. Remember?

CHARLIE. It was the proudest day of my life.

MARGARET MARY. You looked really handsome in it . . . I looked nice too, I suppose.

MANDY. Can I see it, Margaret Mary?

CHARLIE. It's a good suit.

MAX. It is a good suit. I've had a wee look at it myself.

MARGARET MARY. We wanted the best didn't we.

CHARLIE. It was a symbol of the way we wanted things to be wasn't it.

MARGARET MARY. Remember our wedding? Remember the downpour when we came out of the chapel? Downpour? It was like a sea dropped on us! Remember? By the time we got into the cars the bridesmaids dresses were transparent, they were crying, I was crying, my mammie was crying. The rain! Then my uncle Peter stood up at the reception and sang 'Pennies From Heaven'. Remember? So that was it: my Aunt Celine walked out on him there and then. She ended up in Australia eventually, at her sister's. Remember? Then Uncle Peter went and died and Aunt Celine sent us a postcard.

Beat.

CHARLIE. Listen: thanks, MM.

MARGARET MARY. Uch! You can go and visit your mammie now, looking half-decent.

CHARLIE. Listen: thanks, OK? At a time like this ye need reminded.

MARGARET MARY. I better go to the shop, get some confetti. Och (y'know). Nice. Let me see you in your suit before you go, OK?

MARGARET MARY *exits in the direction of the shops.*

MANDY. Come on then, Charlie.

ANN. Where's he going?

MANDY. You can get changed in my room.

ANN. Let me see if he's got everything, Mandy.

MANDY. See what?

ANN. See men! She's put a freshly ironed shirt in there for him.

MANDY. Some people would give up.

ANN. She tries doesn't she. She's a trier.

There's been no visible struggle but ANN *now sets off with the suit.*

ANN. Come on, Charlie: we can get changed together.

MANDY. He can use my room if he wants.

ANN. He can use the boys' bedroom.

MANDY. He can use either.

ANN. He can use the boys' bedroom, Mandy. The last time I opened the door to her room Charlie she had a fox in there!

MANDY. A fox?

ANN. I couldn't believe it either, Charlie, the smell was inedible.

BILLY 2 *enters the back-green to retrieve his suitcases.*

BILLY 2. I've come to get my suitcases, Ann.

ANN. OK, Billy.

BILLY 2. You better go and get ready, Ann.

ANN. OK, Billy. Come on, Charlie.

ANN *exits towards the house.*

MAX. I'll be keeping my eye on ye, Charlie. That suit's your one possible possession. I don't want to lose ye. OK?

MANDY. Charlie. I don't want to lose ye either.

CHARLIE *exits in the direction of the house.* MAX *retreats in the direction of the shops, to somewhere he can cover all exits.*

BILLY 2. I've just come to get my suitcases, Mandy. Then I'll go. Ahch, just disappear is the best thing. – How y' doing anyway, wee man?

MANDY. Och . . .

BILLY 2. Because you tend to get a wee bit forgotten at times. How y' feeling?

MANDY. Och . . .

BILLY 2. Ahch, I'm no too bad. Some ways (now it's happened) I feel more calmer or more tranquiller or more serene, like when I walked out of my bus-crash into that field of cows. How you feeling?

MANDY. Och . . .

BILLY 2. Yeah, I know: I'm as bewildered as you are by it. – She says she still wants to see me though.

MANDY. Listen: if I don't see ye again, all the best.

BILLY 2. Treasure.

> MANDY *exits in the direction of the house.* BILLY 2 *wanders over to the back-green wardrobe, leans against it. A strong light comes onto the wardrobe in the boys' bedroom.*

BILLY 2. The way you touched me, Ann. The sex, Ann. Was the sex too good, is that it? Was it too much? I'm sorry Ann if it was too much at times . . . your nipples are the highest I've been. Or is it because I don't know many words? Because I'm too sensible? If I could only get out of (I'm in a lift. I'm in a high-rise. I'm in a lift in a high-rise. I get out different floors. Four doors. Back in the lift. I wish I was a horse on glue I'd kick more pints of blood out that lift than it knew it had!) If I could only get out of my mind! Would you love me then? I try. I want to. The views would be something else. I nearly can. I can hear but I can't see. A screaming flock of voices? You calling 'Billy! Billy!' – The horse is true, Ann. These kids found it in a field. They put some of their glue in a plastic bag, Ann, used it as a nose-bag. Then they stuck the horse in our lift. They both got broken, Ann.

> *He takes off his tie and makes it into a noose.*

Why I'm doing this, Ann . . . because I'm broken, Ann and . . . just to be the closest to you I can be . . .

> BILLY 2 *goes inside the back-green wardrobe.*

> ANN *and* CHARLIE *come in the boys' bedroom.*

ANN. This is the boys' bedroom.

CHARLIE. Right.

ANN. Uh huh.

CHARLIE. Right.

ANN. This is where the boys slept.

CHARLIE. Is it OK to sit on the beds?

ANN. Yes!

> *They continue to stand.*

ANN. I better go and get ready.

CHARLIE. I spoke to Mandy. It was good, Ann. She helped me to see 'What am I looking for?' Right? Why all the questions? I know all I need to know. What a good feeling. I know all I need to know.

ANN. I've told Billy and Stuart to go out the back and wait. I won't be long.

CHARLIE. Right.

> ANN *goes*. CHARLIE *starts to get changed into his suit.*

> BILLY 1 *and* STUART *enter the back-green from the direction of the house.* BILLY 1 *crosses the entire stage, making sure the other* BILLY *has gone.*

BILLY 1. He's gone. He's gone and left his suitcases. – I think Ann will go through with it now. Eh? D'you think she'll go through with it?

STUART. I hope so, Billy. I hope so.

> *Then they start waiting: whistling, jiggling keys or coins or whatevers in their pockets.*

BILLY 1. Listen to that.

STUART. What?

BILLY 1. Nothing. The day. What time's it?

STUART. Late.

BILLY 1. This time of day (day like today) the day's got no memory. Kids. Wee weans. Remember? We used to spend hours. – What time's your big date?

STUART. It's no a date, Billy.

BILLY 1. You said it was a date.

STUART. I was kidding. I'm having someone round to my flat.

BILLY 1. Yeah?

STUART. And cooking for them. Which is why the time.

> *They wait some more.*

BILLY 1. Who?

STUART. It's no a date, Billy. It's a man.

BILLY 1. Good enough.

STUART. He's a very pleasant, very young, naive young Catholic man I met on a train-journey in Morocco. Anyway he phoned me up to say he's going through a crisis of some kind and could we meet up.

BILLY 1. I see. Are you hoping to turn him?

STUART. Eh?

BILLY 1. Are you hoping to convert him? If he's a naive young Catholic . . .

STUART. I don't think I'd want to change that, Billy . . . (We all go our own sweet way to perdition.)

Inside the boys' bedroom, CHARLIE, suit on, a new man, raises his hand to knock on the wardobe door when someone knocks on the bedroom door.

CHARLIE. Who is it?

ANN. It's Ann. Can I come in?

CHARLIE. Come on in, Ann.

ANN comes in, wearing her wedding outfit, and closes the door behind her.

ANN. They're waiting on me.

CHARLIE. You look great.

ANN. You look great too.

CHARLIE. Like a bride and groom.

ANN. Is it OK to sit on the bed?

CHARLIE. Yeah!

ANN. I come here a lot.

CHARLIE. Sit.

ANN. Sit.

CHARLIE. Think.

ANN. Think.

CHARLIE. 'Why?'

ANN. Or think about 'a person'.

CHARLIE. A person?

ANN. Is that what I want to be? (I don't think a person's very applicable nowadays.) She's a person, supposedly. Mandy. Or she tries. She beavers away like a fox. – She hates me coming here. She stands outside and listens. Listen.

CHARLIE looks at the bedroom door, listens.

ANN. I don't say nothing. I keep her hanging on.

CHARLIE. I like Mandy, to be truthful.

ANN. She haunts me. – Martin used to come here a lot too. After his brother hung himself. That big effn wardrobe spoke to him. So Martin said. He heard voices. – Faithfulness. That's what Martin teaches us. He wanted to be with his brother didn't he. I've said that to Mandy. After Martin went and hung himself? She went and took against him, I had to say to her, 'He wanted to be with his brother, Mandy!' – Martin came back from the dead and explained everything. He explained he was dead and Robert was dead too. I said, 'Oh Martin, explain to me!' He said 'I've explained.' It was good though, we stayed up all night having a laugh. I kept thinking he'd go, I kept thinking 'He's going to go!' Then the ceiling fell in. I thought I was dreaming but no, I was found on the floor bleeding from the ears and a cracked skull to ponder. The ceiling was good as new though.

CHARLIE. Who found you?

Silence. CHARLIE *looks again at the bedroom door.*

ANN. The dead are like kids, Charlie. The dead are like wee kids. They don't know the difference between one thing and another. A pavement? That's something to play with. They pull bricks out the pavement and dump them on the road don't they. A fence is another thing. A fence is a joke round here. They laugh at a fence. They take things apart till you can't tell the difference between one thing and another. – Come here and sit beside me.

CHARLIE *crosses and sits on the bed.*

CHARLIE. Ann . . . . . . any way I can console you Ann . . . You're no ugly, that's one thing I will say.

ANN. Oh Charlie . . . What am I going to do now . . .

CHARLIE. Whatever, Ann . . .

ANN. What's my instincts telling me?

CHARLIE. Maybe just . . . no to think too much . . .

ANN. I suppose we're all only skin deep. I'm glad you like Mandy.

CHARLIE. I like Mandy.

ANN. She used to be lovely. I'd look at her when she was wee, when she was asleep. You know how: tulips at night, when they close up? Uch, I suppose she's still lovely.

CHARLIE. She's nice. She's nice enough. She's a nice person.

ANN. She wants to save you.

CHARLIE. She wants to save me from . . .

ANN. . . . . save you for . . .

CHARLIE. . . . save me from . . .

ANN . . . sin . . .

CHARLIE. . . . yeah? . . .

ANN. . . . is that what you want? . . .

CHARLIE. . . . sin? . . .

ANN. . . . mmm . . .

CHARLIE. . . . we all want to be good . . .

ANN. . . . I know . . .

CHARLIE. . . . we maybe just don't know how . . .

ANN. . . . what's my instincts telling me? They've all gone away and fled . . .

CHARLIE. . . . yeah? . . .

ANN. . . . yeah . . .

CHARLIE *touches* ANN. ANN *moves into him.*

CHARLIE. . . . what are we doing? . . .

ANN *and* CHARLIE *start kissing.*

ANN. . . . what's happening? . . .

CHARLIE. . . . I don't know . . .

ANN. . . . I can't remember what's even happening . . .

ANN *and* CHARLIE *are now climbing all over each other. They look as if they're heading for wild sex . . . erogenous zones are being handled . . .*

MANDY *comes through the bedroom door.*

MANDY. Right you: out!

ANN. Mandy!

MANDY. Out!

ANN. Oh she's ugly, oh she's ugly! Oh look, I've left half my face on Charlie.

MANDY. You can put your face back on, on the way.

ANN. How do I look, Charlie?

CHARLIE. Ugly. I'm kidding. You look fine, Ann.

ANN. Are you sure?

CHARLIE. Yeah.

ANN. Wish me all the best then.

CHARLIE. I wish you all the best, Ann.

ANN *goes*.

MANDY. Wish us all the best, Charlie.

CHARLIE. I wish you all the (so I'm – what? – I'm something to be torn apart by horses? – yeah?)

MANDY *goes out the bedroom door*.

Out the back-green . . .

BILLY 1. Has it gone dark?

STUART. Patience, Billy, patience: (we'll all be in glory soon enough).

CHARLIE *goes out the bedroom door*.

PROPHET JOHN *enters the back-green with a mattress and some bed-sheets, followed by* NANETTE.

NANETTE. John, I'm beginning to lose my patience, John, where are you going with Ann's sheets!

PROPHET JOHN *starts making up a bed*.

NANETTE. John, what on earth are you playing at! John, I think we should go, John. I came here hoping for a wedding as I'm sure Billy did and I'm no staying for a lot of carry-on. We're guests here.

PROPHET JOHN *goes to shake* STUART'*s hand*.

PROPHET JOHN. Can I shake your hand, pastor? Can I shake your hand, pastor? Can I shake your hand, pastor?

They shake. PROPHET JOHN *holds* STUART *in his grasp*.

PROPHET JOHN (*to* STUART). My bride has many names. She was taken from her bed in the secret of the night, and driven from the land, herself and her handmaidens and her counsellors. I know her as Asherah. I've prepared a marriage-bed.

NANETTE. Ahch, yir arse in parsley! C'mon, John, c'mon, we're going, we're off, quick before Ann comes out here and obliterates you or I do it for her! – Oh, smelly knickers: too late, here she comes. Here comes the bride.

MARGARET MARY *and* MAX *enter the back-green from the direction of the shops*.

BILLY 1. Ann?

NANETTE. She's on her way.

BILLY 1. Oh god. So she is.

MARGARET MARY. What's happening?

NANETTE. Surprise! There's going to be a wedding after all.

BILLY 1. Can we get lined up then! Can we get into some kind of order here instead of standing around looking surprised!

They get into a line-up of sorts; NANETTE starts dah-dah-dahing the bridal march and PROPHET JOHN awaits his bride.

ANN enters at speed, followed by MANDY.

ANN. I'm here, I'm here.

MARGARET MARY. Awwwww.

BILLY 1. Ann, you look – glorious.

ANN. Do I.

MARGARET MARY. So she does.

ANN. For once.

BILLY 1. Not for once.

ANN. Not for long.

STUART. Will we get lined up then?

MAX. Where's Charlie, has he sneaked off? Eh? Because I know Charlie, and I can tell you he's a hole for snakes.

STUART. OK, Billy?

BILLY 1. I'm –

STUART. OK, Ann?

BILLY 1. – ecstatic.

ANN. Quick, before I'm old.

They are now more or less lined up. PROPHET JOHN has placed himself beside ANN like he's the groom.

STUART. We'll keep it short. Ann, Billy, want to get married and here we are. The bride's lovely, the groom's a fine-looking man, it's a lovely day. What do I know? The great thing is: we hope.

ANN. Did you invite your fat pal, Mandy?

MANDY. No.

ANN. Naw. I'm her only interest in life.

STUART. Hope, like Noah's dove sent out upon the face of the Flood; hope which, without it there is no living. A wedding is all about hope. We hope maybe for a happy ending or maybe we hope to do something that will stand for all time.

ANN. Her fat pal's no even her pal, she's just a big fat stupit lassie. You don't see her for months and then you come home from work and there's ugly lying on the couch under a duvet and six empty cans of diet coke, feeling sorry for herself. How many abortions does she intend to have?

STUART. And yet nothing stands for all time. Everything, thankfully, passes. So spend your days with the one you love, all the lovely futile days God gives you under the sun.

STUART *now moves to the service proper and a slightly less casual more solemn tone.*

STUART. Unless the Lord builds the house, those who build it labour in vain. Billy, Ann, we have come here in the presence of God and these witnesses so you can be joined in marriage. As God made a covenant with his people in the desert so now you will make a covenant with each other. This is not something to be entered into lightly or unadvisedly but thoughtfully and reverently. Cherish today and the vows you are about to make.

This man and this woman are about to pledge themselves before God and man. I therefore ask you all – if you know any reason why this man and this woman may not lawfully be joined in marriage to speak now since no one speaks, let us ask God's blessing on this union. Almighty Father –

MARGARET MARY. Can we stop this?

ANN. It's like –

BILLY 1. Like what?

ANN. Like. Does anyone else feel it? Like the sun's fell off his chariot in the sky.

NANETTE. I think maybe.

ANN. Is someone missing?

MANDY. Is it you do you think?

ANN. Apart from me.

STUART. It's not too late to stop.

ANN. No! I'm just saying.

STUART. Billy, if you'd like to take Ann's hand – and say after me the words of the covenant. I, William Shearer –

PROPHET JOHN. I do.

STUART. I, William Shearer –

CHARLIE *enters from the direction of the house in a dionysiac rage.*

CHARLIE. I've just come to say I'm off. I'm off, Ann. I'm off, Mandy.

ANN. OK, Charlie.

CHARLIE. OK?

ANN. OK. See you again mibby.

CHARLIE. OK. Max, are you coming, son? (I feel sorry for you
Billy, I fucking pity you to fuck). C'mon, Max: let's get out of
here: because the one *good* thing about Max (someone dipped
the evil bastard in poison) he's a lying fuck but fuck me
(I mean it) Max *lies* . . .

ANN. . . . (don't, Charlie) . . .

CHARLIE. . . . Max is steeped, but he's never deceived me, Ann,
he's never deceived me Mandy, he's never led me on to believe,
Mandy, or led me into a bedroom Ann and played with me, or
tore me in two. I'm no saying I like the jobby fuck and there's a
side to Max I don't like but yeah. Yes. Absolutely. Yes! How
close I am to Max, Billy, I once hospitalised the cunt . . .

BILLY 1. . . . (what's going on) . . .

CHARLIE. . . . once hospitalised the cunt. It was his idea. I agreed,
I said fine. We were skint so right so fine so OK we go out to
look for a shop to rob . . .

STUART. . . . (look, Charlie, do ye mind) . . .

CHARLIE. . . . you can put this in a sermon, Stuart. So we go
under the motorway and past the gasworks across . . .

MARGARET MARY. . . . (glory be) . . .

CHARLIE. . . . across terrain more suited to the camel until we
gets to the local shopping-centre. The problem being society,
the shops where we live have all been burnt to a crisp or
scalped or fucking *robbed* . . .

NANETTE. . . . (glory) . . .

CHARLIE. . . . we gets to the shopping-centre (I get angry about
this). The lack of choice is a scandal even from the shopping
point of view. They've got a half-shut Paki shop.

Time. (This is about three weeks ago.)

We're watching the Paki shop.

Time.

When I'm angry I show it, Billy (one of my good points).

I *know* the Paki. I go there for my bread, fags don't I. His name's
Hami, he's an Indian.

What Time is, Time's an explosion . . . naw, *explosion* and then
what Time is, Time's meantime.

I goes, 'Max, you want me to go *in* there?' He goes, 'Yes.'
I goes, 'You want me to go *in* there and rob him with nothing
but my bare hands?' Max goes, 'Pretend it's not you.'

CHARLIE *snaps his fingers.*

CHARLIE. Aw man. I . . . *went.* I crossed the Jordan. I . . . whhhho! I . . . went. There was no nothing, no sky, no ground, no Time. Or like . . . Time. It was . . . alleluia . . . it was . . . what's the word, what's the word . . . good. Across the Jordan . . .

CHARLIE *snaps his fingers.*

. . . then you come back. I look down and there's Max like the skin off some dead animal, like a fucking pelt. I'd very near mauled him to death. I'd very near killed him with my bare hands, Billy. – So d'you get me, Billy? Am I in disguise some kind, some kinna cloak. I've came out here Billy, I've came out here Ann, cloaked in violence, cloaked in violence, to scatter the truth to fuck! The reality is, Billy. And that's the reality.

BILLY 1 *finds* ANN, *who's wishing she was invisible somewhere.*

BILLY 1 (*shell-shocked*). Ann, after all my best efforts . . . ? – I'm on the verge here . . . – So did something mibby happen you can't explain while I was out here with Stuart waiting to get married . . . ? – Are we food for the gods, is that it . . . ?

ANN. Don't look at me, Billy'

BILLY 1. I don't know where to look . . . Nobody does . . .

ANN. Charlie?

CHARLIE. Yeah?

ANN *crosses to him.*

ANN. Oh Charlie. How can I say it? It's a hellish mess and I don't want to be here either. You said it better than me. You shone. I want to go, 'cross' . . .

CHARLIE. Cross . . .

ANN. Across . . .

CHARLIE. To.

ANN. You can take my face off. Across where pretend who's not me . . . Across and murder the whole contents of my brain and hang them from the branches of a tree and have a laugh. And yeah. You know? Yes! And no come back.

CHARLIE. You want to . . . cross the shining river . . .

ANN. And no come back.

CHARLIE. And no come back.

ANN. You can pick my bones.

Three slow dull knocks come from inside the back-green wardrobe. Everyone has a near heart-attack.

ANN. Oh god.

MARGARET MARY. Oh god.

ANN. Oh god.

Three more slow dull knocks.

ANN. Oh god. Who is it? Oh god. Who'll hide me?

BILLY 1. I'll go and look, Ann.

BILLY 1 *goes to open the wardrobe door.* ANN *picks up a stone, to protect herself.*

ANN. You'd better watch it, Martin! D'you think this is an ugly mask I've got on? Try taking it off then! Try taking it bloody off and I'll show you ugly will turn to stone! I'm infested, I'm multiplying, I'm snakes, I'm Legion. It's you that can't look at me, it's you that can't bear to look at me!

BILLY 1 *opens the wardrobe door.* ANN *sees Martin. Or rather,* ANN *hallucinates Martin. The anger that's released in her is powerful, free-flowing and channelled directly against Martin.*

At some point during her next speech BILLY 2 *steps out of the wardrobe, with the tie tied around his neck, and starts walking towards her.*

ANN. Martin! Martin, ya wee snake! Ya wee rat! You can go right back down that tunnel! You can go right back down that tunnel, son! What do you want now? The skin off my back? The bones I stand up in? You've already got them, you've already taken them away and buried them, son! Don't you come near me, don't you come near me – or I swear to God I will let the dogs tear you apart.

CHARLIE. Who'll strike the first blow?

PROPHET JOHN. We all will.

MAX. I'll pelt him!

NANETTE. I'll obliterate him!

MANDY. Stupid old creep!

MARGARET MARY. I'll bloody wedding him!

MARGARET MARY *throws her confetti at him, violently.*

BILLY 2. Ann, Ann –

ANN. Get away!

BILLY 2. It's me, Ann. It's Billy.

ANN. Who?

BILLY 2. Billy. I tried my best Ann. I wanted to just be the closest I could be to you. I used my tie Ann. It broke Ann. I'm sorry.

ANN *is well out of it. Apparently she can't even trust her eyes. She feels ugly. She feels hellish ugly.*

CHARLIE. Can I help you, Ann?

ANN. Who are you? Eh? Who are you?

CHARLIE. Charlie, Ann.

ANN *doesn't seem to know a* CHARLIE.

ANN. Charlie?

CHARLIE. You need help, Ann.

ANN. I don't know a Charlie. Will you do me a favour, Charlie? You know the big hanging thing in the boys' bedroom? Will you take it away for me? You're the only one I can ask, Charlie.

CHARLIE. Now?

ANN. Oh please Charlie, save my life.

Pause.

CHARLIE. Come on, Max: follow me.

CHARLIE *exits in the direction of the house.* MAX *goes after him.*

NANETTE *and* STUART *are round* ANN. ANN's *putting on some fresh make-up.*

MARGARET MARY. Is she OK? Are you OK, Ann? Is she OK? Is that it? Are you OK, father? Is Ann OK? It's OK, I'll be fine in a minute. I'll be fine in a minute, Mandy.

ANN *is still fixing her face. When she says the next line it's not clear which of the* BILLYS *she's addressing.*

ANN. Billy, this is the last I want to see you. I've made my decision. I love Billy. I love Billy to bits. I only went out with you to confuse things and once I started I got all mixed up. I wanted to be fair to the both of you (oh god, what a mess) . . . I knew I was cheating on the two of ye and I wanted to make up for it by showing ye I was a horrible lying cow that wasn't worth bothering about anyway. Then, as time went on, I lost my flavour.

She's crying.

ANN. I'm sorry, Billy. I tried to tell you. I thought you might take the hint when I told you I was getting married to Billy but no. I suppose I led you to believe (which I was, I was!) I was scared. I was scared witless. I was really scared, Billy. I was frightened in case everything worked out the way I wanted them to, and what would I do then?

CHARLIE *and* MAX *enter the boys' bedroom.*

BILLY 2. I'm sorry, Ann. I wanted to carry your burden, Ann. I'm no very clever, Ann, but I can lift heavy things: and all I ever wanted was to put all your sadness in a box, Ann, and carry it away, even supposing it was heavier than plutonium, Ann: which, it would be, Ann, it would be. – What I would say, Ann: if you really want me to go, if you want me to believe you, say it to my face.

CHARLIE and MAX carry the wardrobe out of the boys' bedroom.

ANN turns and looks at BILLY 2.

ANN. I want you to go, Billy.

BILLY 2 starts to exit in the direction of the shops. As he does so ANN's fear mounts: it looks like everything is going to turn out the way she wants them to and what will she do then?

ANN. Billy!

BILLY 2 stops.

What if everything turns out the way I want them to?

BILLY 2. I hope they do, Ann.

BILLY 2 exits.

BILLY 1. I knew, Ann, when the day was over you'd look back and see, deep down you were only ever faithful to me.

ANN. Oh Billy.

STUART. Will we leave you two alone to talk?

ANN. No! I want to ask Billy a question.

BILLY 1. You ask me any question you want the answer's the same, Ann: I love you.

ANN. Billy, will you stop trying to scare me away like a ghost!

When she asks BILLY the question ANN seems almost to be looking more at MANDY, as if she's asking her the question as well.

Suppose I was ever to be happy, Billy. Suppose I was ever happy. Would you despise me?

BILLY 1. No.

ANN. Would you hate me?

BILLY 1. No.

ANN. You wouldn't loathe me?

BILLY 1. No, Ann.

ANN. I'm no saying I will be happy. I'm just saying suppose I was. I mean, it's been nine year now. It's been nine year now hasn't it, Stuart.

STUART. Nine years, Ann.

ANN. They'd have grown up and left me by now. The thing is I made them a promise when they died: I swore I'd never forgive myself and I've been true as my word. So if I was ever to be happy; which, I'm no saying I will be, Mandy; I'm only raising the spectre that I might be –

MANDY turns on her heels and walks off in the direction of the house.

Mandy! Will you get back here! Do you think I don't feel guilty enough as it is, I'm guilty as all hell!

ANN sees CHARLIE and MAX off, coming with the wardrobe.

ANN. Oh and look who's coming to cheer me up, my two undertakers. Billy, will you stand next to me. Stuart, will you stand next to me.

BILLY 1 and STUART stand next to ANN.

CHARLIE and MAX enter carrying the wardrobe.

CHARLIE. Is Mandy OK? She seems a wee bit upset.

ANN. She's a wee bit upset, Charlie.

CHARLIE. It's just that she seems a wee bit upset, y'know.

ANN. She'll be fine.

CHARLIE. Are you OK?

ANN. I'll be fine. (If I don't fall to pieces.)

CHARLIE. We'll be fine.

ANN. Thanks for doing your undertaker, Charlie. Will you promise me something?

CHARLIE. Of course Ann.

ANN. I don't want to see that dumped somewhere, vandalised the middle of the road or some back-green.

CHARLIE. I'm disappointed you can say that, Ann.

ANN. And I don't want to see you again either.

Beat.

CHARLIE. Come on, Max. It looks like we're on our own, son.

MAX. Looks like it, Charlie.

CHARLIE. Come on, Max. We better go son.

MAX. On you go then son.

CHARLIE doesn't move.

CHARLIE. I wish you all the best Ann. Today (to draw a line) it's no been all bad. Many many ways I've succeeded. I've prepared myself and underchanged my thoughts. And now that I've done as much as I can here, which, I think I have done Ann, I can go on from here. OK, Max?

MAX. I'll follow you, my friend.

CHARLIE *and* MAX *carry the wardrobe off in the direction of the shops. As the wardrobe passes,* MARGARET MARY *makes the sign of the cross and bows her head while* STUART *and Billy hold* ANN, *who physically shrinks, as at the interment of a loved one. Nobody speaks till the wardrobe is gone.*

BILLY 1. Would you maybe say a few words, Stuart . . . ?

STUART. . . . a few words . . . ?

BILLY 1. . . . I thought you might oblige us with a few words of comfort . . .

STUART. Would we no be better getting a drink down us, Billy! I've been on the go since seven this morning, I've hardly been off my feet yet, I've had poverty drugs depression bereavement bronchitis and sheer bloody misery all day and I've still to write tomorrow's sermon preaching the good news.

ANN. I've still got Mandy to face.

STUART. OK, Ann; let's get you inside.

ANN. Ask Margaret Mary in for a drink, will ye Billy.

BILLY 1. Margaret Mary, will you come in for a drink?

MARGARET MARY. OK. – I wanted there to be a wedding so much.

BILLY 1. There might be a wedding yet. – Stuart, will you stay and have a drink, Stuart? I mean, you won't run off and leave us?

STUART. It's OK, Billy: I'll phone my friend and cancel him.

BILLY 1. Thanks, Stuart. Because we're nearly there. We're nearly there, Ann. We're very nearly there, Margaret Mary. – Love. Love will find a way.

Like people after an interment, ANN, STUART, BILLY *and* MARGARET MARY *drift off in the direction of the house.*

NANETTE *wants to go with the others but first she has to get rid of* JOHN. *She goes and picks up* ANN's *sheets.*

NANETTE. You're some piece of work, John. I won't blaspheme by saying you were put together so badly nothing will make you right again. I hope in God and I hope you walk in his light one day but I never want to see the outside of your face or the inside of your mind for as long as I have breath.

NANETTE *exits in the direction of the house carrying the sheets.* PROPHET JOHN *exits the other way.*

MANDY *enters the boys' bedroom.*

The summer afternoon turns into a summer's evening.

It's now about ten o'clock, so it's still light outside. Maybe we hear the sounds of a long summer night, wee boys and girls still playing in the streets after a long hard day of it, but mostly quiet.

MANDY*'s sitting on the bed in the boys' bedroom. Outside the door is* ANN.

ANN. Mandy! Will you come out of there? Everybody's still waiting. They're all round at Margaret Mary's house waiting on us. – I'm sorry about Charlie. I don't know what that was all about. You know how when you get something stuck in your teeth? – Mandy? Are you on your own in there? – We can't Mandy on like this. We can't Robert Martin for good. That's what Charlie teaches us. We're too stuck together. – Is it because I said I might be happy?

ANN *enters the boys' bedroom.*

ANN. Is it because I said I might be happy? – I didn't mean it, Mandy. I admit it's crossed my mind that maybe the time has come to maybe foresee a future, which is why I like to get my cards read. I admit I maybe hoped, I do admit that. But as quick as I hoped I just as quick despaired, Mandy, and that's the gospel truth. – You know me, Mandy: I believe a lot of rubbish. I even believe in happy endings. Do you not? Do you not believe in happy endings, Mandy?

MANDY. Are you fucking stupit!

ANN. Mandy!

MANDY. Eh? Are you stupit, ya dippit cow!

ANN. I've never denied I'm stupid.

MANDY. I've carried you for nine years, ya mongol! I've had dreams about it, dreams where I'm carrying this big mongol over my shoulder like a big stupit carpet and the mongol's crying and I can taste his tears in my mouth, these warm tears, and I try to spit them out without him seeing. I've had nine years of it. And now you want to get married and live happy ever after? If you're going to be somebody else, who am I going to be! – There are rules. There have to be rules. Otherwise how will I know you're you, ya Martian. – You're you and I'm me; you're weak and I'm strong; you despair and I hope; I lead and you follow; that's the rules and if we keep the rules,

if we keep the rules, if we don't keep the rules then it's
pandemonium. I don't like you any more than you do: I don't
want to be me either: I don't want to be me any more than you
want to be you: but I accept my responsibilities. That's the way
things are and we just have to get on with it.

ANN (*fierce*). Right you: out! This is the end. I don't care if it's
happy or no I just want an end so as I can start and if Billy's
going to be daft enough to marry me the least I can do is try to
be happy. If I try for long enough maybe I'll get the hang of it
again.

*The unfortunate turn of phrase reminds her of the boys'
wardrobe and she looks guiltily in the direction where the
wardrobe used to be.*

ANN. I mean, I'll maybe get into the swing of it again. – Oh, I
give up.

*ANN crosses over and sits on the bed, suddenly tired and
defeated.*

MANDY. So they're all round at Margaret Mary's.

ANN. I can't get married here.

MANDY. So they're all round at Margaret Mary's.

ANN. Margaret Mary said why not have the ceremony in her house.

They sit there.

MANDY. I don't like sudden changes.

*CHARLIE and MAX enter the back-green from the direction
of the shops. CHARLIE crosses the extent of the back-green.*

He shouts up at the house.

CHARLIE. Mandy! Mandy!

In the boys' bedroom . . .

ANN. How are we ever going to get out of here?

MANDY. Do you want to?

ANN. If you want to.

MANDY. OK. On you go then.

ANN. OK.

Neither of them move.

ANN. It's just that Stuart's been very patient.

MANDY. On you go then.

Uncertainly, ANN stands up.

ANN. Come on then.

*MANDY gets to her feet and actually moves part of the way
across the room.*

ANN. Are we going?

    MANDY *stops dead.*

MANDY. I think so.

    ANN *starts to move across the room towards the door, moving with blind courage.*

MANDY. Are we going then?

    ANN *stops dead.*

ANN. We seem to be.

MANDY. D'you think I'll ever have a baby?

ANN. Do you want a baby?

MANDY. I'd probably get pregnant then lose it. I can't seem to hang on to anything.

    Beat.

ANN. I'll still miss them, Mandy.

    ANN *goes out the bedroom door.* MANDY *follows.*

    Out the back-green . . .

CHARLIE. Mandy!

    A big dog barks in the distance. CHARLIE *turns round, sees* MAX *is still there.*

CHARLIE. You still here?

MAX. You know I am.

    CHARLIE *takes off his suit jacket. He walks over to* MAX, *holds it out to him.*

CHARLIE. There. Take it.

MAX. Eh?

CHARLIE. Take it.

MAX. What does this mean?

CHARLIE. Take it.

MAX. You're asking me to take it?

CHARLIE. Correct.

MAX. Are you 'giving' it to me?

CHARLIE. Yes.

MAX. What happens if I take it?

CHARLIE. Take it and see.

MAX. I'm anticipating.

    CHARLIE *drops it, turns his back and walks away.*

MAX. Charlie, have I upset you in some way? Is it to do with the seasons? Look, I apologise if I spoke my mind, ya huffy cunt.

OK? I'm sorry. Naw, I'm no sorry, why should I be sorry, at least I speak what's in my mind. You, I have to pull your insides out and read your entrails, ya omen.

MAX *indicates the jacket.*

Here's an example. A jacket? What's that mean? That's no use to me.

CHARLIE. Take it, ya jackal.

MAX. I mean, I pick that up (I'm anticipating) I pick that up (that's immaterial to me) I even so much as pick that up before I even so much as picked that up Time would come to an end rather than watch or look on or even countenance an act so abject as to be beneath a maggot. And if you think I'm capable of that Charlie then maybe the time has come to go our separate ways.

CHARLIE. OK.

MAX. OK?

CHARLIE. OK, leave the jacket and fuck off.

MAX. OK. Fine. – What about tonight? – It's dark getting. It's a bit late to be out hunting somewhere to stay. – You're welcome to come back to the house.

CHARLIE. I'll be OK.

MAX. You can't sleep out, Charlie.

CHARLIE. I'll make a hole.

Beat.

MAX. OK, well you know where I am, Charlie. – I never anticipated this. I never anticipated I'd be saying adios amigo. – Anyway, you know where I am, Charlie. I'll be back at the house waiting on ye.

CHARLIE*'s still not looking at him.* MAX *has no alternative but to just go.*

CHARLIE *sees* MANDY *and* ANN *on their way to* MARGARET MARY*'s and calls over to them.*

CHARLIE. Mandy! Come here a minute.

MANDY (offstage). We've only got a minute.

CHARLIE. This'll only take a minute.

MANDY *enters from the direction of the house, fairly closely accompanied by* ANN.

CHARLIE. How's the wee barra?

MANDY. No bad.

CHARLIE. How's the wee barra? Come over here, till I have a wee word with you.

CHARLIE *wants to detach* MANDY *from* ANN.

MANDY. You'll have to be quick, we're going to get married.

CHARLIE. The both of ye?

MANDY. Yeah.

CHARLIE. You're getting married too?

MANDY. We're both going to get her married – Margaret Mary said we could have the ceremony in her house.

CHARLIE. I've come to get the day. Get the day in some kind of perspective. My mammie died, sadly.

MANDY. Aw.

CHARLIE. Yeah. I never seen her. We'll get the body back on Monday. So . . .

MANDY. What's your favourite part of the body?

CHARLIE. Whose body?

MANDY. Your body.

CHARLIE. I don't have one.

MANDY. Everybody has a body. I like my neck.

ANN. Mandy! What a thing to say!

MANDY. I quite like my eyes now that I've found my tones. I take blues and pinks and sunsets, any colour you see in the sky. She's earth. She's more brown and green.

Beat.

CHARLIE. Today (to get the day) I've had worse days thankfully. I've admired your christian breastplate of faith. There was even a moment today when I was happy. You led me to believe . . . And I believed.

MANDY. Good.

CHARLIE. Do you believe me?

MANDY. Uh huh.

CHARLIE. And . . . I felt (that) I was no longer alone. Y' know?

MANDY. Yeah.

CHARLIE. Y' know?

MANDY. You're too sad and old for me.

Slight pause.

CHARLIE. I'm disappointed you can say that. I am. How can you say that? Fuck. Y' know? I'm describing a moment Christian when I felt like an effing Christian. Don't forsake me that moment when – when – as I remember it, as I remember it –

I no longer wanted to strike anyone. My blood stopped clawing me; and I was glad enough for two.

MANDY. Aw, that's nice.

CHARLIE. I was glad enough for two.

MANDY. We have to go.

CHARLIE. I have to go too.

MANDY. OK.

CHARLIE. Tell me to be good.

MANDY. Be good.

CHARLIE. I will, I will. And you take care now, you see and take care.

MANDY. I'll say a wee prayer for you.

> MANDY *turns to* ANN, *smiles.*

MANDY. Are you excited yet?

ANN. No! Don't be daft!

MANDY. Are you not excited? I am.

ANN. I'm too tense.

> *Suddenly* MANDY *throws some confetti over* ANN. ANN *squeals in excitement, fear, concern for her hair, clothes.*

MANDY (*sings*). Over yonder valley
Where the green grass grows
Sits Ann Fairley
Washing all her clothes
And she sang and she sang
And she sang so sweet
She sang Billy Shearer
Across the street.

> ANN *joins in the second verse. Then, as* ANN *tries to get the confetti out of her clothes,* MANDY *exits. The tension between them over* CHARLIE *has now completely evaporated.*

MANDY. C'mawn, mammie! We'll be late!

ANN. Wait for me, Mandy! – Oh god. Oh god. Oh god. Oh Billy darlin', I'm coming, I'm coming.

CHARLIE. Will you tell Margaret Mary the bad news?

ANN. Oh uh huh.

CHARLIE. She'll want to know.

ANN. I'll let her know.

CHARLIE. Don't let it spoil your happy event.

ANN. Do I look OK?

CHARLIE. If I was the groom I'd be a happy man.

ANN. Aw, that's nice. Oh Billy darlin', I hope I don't cry too much. All I want is to have one happy day one day.

ANN exits in the direction of the house.

CHARLIE watches till she disappears from his sight. Then he thinks about going away. He doesn't know where to go. He crosses the stage, stops, covers his face. Maybe he sits down.

CHARLIE. 'What is it, Charlie son? Are you OK? You're awfy quiet, son. You were out awfy late. Were you playing football? Ah you stick in, Charlie son, you'll be playing for the Celtic one of these days. You're awfy quiet, son. Was it the nice lady? Did the nice lady scare you? It's OK. She's gone. She'll no come back again, son, I've seen to that. I'm your mammy, son, always have been, always will be. – Have you said your prayers? We'll say a prayer then I'll tuck you in. OK? Will we say a prayer? I'll say the words and you say them after me.'

The words of the prayer are spoken with a pause after each phrase in which we imagine the seven-year-old CHARLIE repeating the words after his mammie/granny.

'Hail, holy queen . . .
mother of mercy . . .
Hail, our life . . .
our sweetness and our hope . . .
To thee do we cry . . .
poor banished children of Eve . . .
To thee do we send up our sighs . . .
mourning and weeping in this vale of tears . . .
Turn then, most gracious advocate . . .
thine eyes of mercy towards us . . .
and after this our exile . . .
show unto us the fruit of thy womb Jesus . . .
O clement . . .
O loving . . .
O sweet Virgin Mary.'

Silence. CHARLIE wipes his eyes. Then gets to his feet and starts to make a move.

Then from offstage there is the sound of applause, pleasure, a happy event.

CHARLIE hears it, stops, looks up in the direction of MARGARET MARY's. Then goes.

It gets dark.

The End.

A Nick Hern Book

Shining Souls first published in Great Britain in 1966
as a paperback original by Nick Hern Books Limited,
14 Larden Road, London W3 7ST, in association with
the Traverse Theatre, Edinburgh

Front cover picture by Euan Myles

Typeset by Country Setting, Woodchurch, Kent TN26 3TB
Printed and bound in Great Britain by Cox and Wyman Ltd,
Reading, Berks

ISBN 1-85459-361-7

A CIP catalogue record for this book is available from
the British Library

This text went to press before the opening night at the Traverse
Theatre and may therefore differ slightly from the play as performed.